Psychic NAVIGATOR

–Also by John Holland

Born Knowing: A Medium's Journey—
Accepting and Embracing My Spiritual Gifts

⊠ ⊠ ⊠

Hay House Titles of Related Interest

Books

After Life, by John Edward
Chakra Clearing (book-with-CD), by Doreen Virtue, Ph.D.
Contacting Your Spirit Guide (book-with-CD), by Sylvia Browne
Getting in the Gap (book-with-CD), by Dr. Wayne W. Dyer
Meditation (book-with-CD), by Brian L. Weiss, M.D.
Spirit Medicine (book-with-CD), by Hank Wesselman, Ph.D.,
and Jill Kuykendall, RPT
Spirit Messenger, by Gordon Smith
Trust Your Vibes, by Sonia Choquette
What Color Is Your Personality? by Carol Ritberger, Ph.D

Card Decks

Heart and Soul, by Sylvia Browne
Trust Your Vibes Oracle Cards, by Sonia Choquette
Wisdom Cards, by Louise L. Hay

All of the above are available at your local bookstore,
or may be ordered by visiting:

Hay House USA: **www.hayhouse.com**®
Hay House Australia: **www.hayhouse.com.au**
Hay House UK: **www.hayhouse.co.uk**
Hay House South Africa: **www.hayhouse.co.za**
Hay House India: **www.hayhouse.co.in**

Harnessing Your Inner Guidance

John Holland

HAY HOUSE, INC.

Carlsbad, California • New York City
London • Sydney • Johannesburg
Vancouver • Hong Kong • New Delhi

Published and distributed in the United States by: Hay House, Inc.: www.
hayhouse.com • **Published and distributed in Australia by:** Hay House
Australia Pty. Ltd.: www.hayhouse.com.au • **Published and distributed in the
United Kingdom by:** Hay House UK, Ltd.: www.hayhouse.co.uk • **Published and
distributed in the Republic of South Africa by:** Hay House SA (Pty), Ltd.: www.
hayhouse.co.za • **Distributed in Canada by:** Raincoast: www.raincoast.com
Published in India by: Hay House Publishers India: www.hayhouse.co.in

Editorial supervision: Jill Kramer
John Holland's editor: Simon Steel
Design: Summer McStravick

Library of Congress Control Number: 2004103922

ISBN 10: 1-4019-0242-1
ISBN 13: 978-1-4019-0242-1

10 09 08 07   7 6 5 4
1st printing, August 2004
4th printing, November 2007

Printed in the United States of America

*This book is dedicated to Spirit; my family,
friends, teachers, and all my students;
and to <u>you</u>, the reader, for taking the
next steps to discover and embrace
all that you truly are and can be.*

CONTENTS

Introduction   xi

CHAPTER 1: YOUR NEVER-ENDING GUIDANCE   1

- What Does *Psychic* Mean?
- Psychic Abilities and Intuition
- The Importance of Learning the Equipment
- Preparing Yourself to Begin

CHAPTER 2: DISCOVERING YOUR PSYCHIC STRENGTHS   21

- Clairsentience
- Clairvoyance
- Clairaudience

CHAPTER 3: INTO THE STILLNESS   39

- What Is Meditation?
- Relaxing the Body and Mind
- Active Meditation
- Accessing Your Higher Mind

CHAPTER 4: THE VITAL FORCE   59

- Breath Awareness
- The Complete Breath
- Mindfulness of Breathing
- Psychic Breathing Techniques

CHAPTER 5: THE HUMAN PSYCHIC ATMOSPHERE   79

- What Is an Aura?
- Developing Auric Vision
- Aura Colors and Their Meanings
- Sensing the Aura
- Strengthening the Aura

CHAPTER 6: SPIRITUAL BATTERIES   107

- What Are Chakras?
- The Seven Energy Centers
- Chakra Workouts
- Raising the Power

CHAPTER 7: PSYCHIC TOOLS FOR LIFE   133

- Decision Making
- Psychometry
- Energy Scanning
- Your Psychic Time

About the Meditation CD   **149**
Afterword   **151**
Recommended Resources   **153**
Acknowledgments   **155**
About the Author   **157**

"Your gifts are like a rose unfolding.
You cannot force the bloom.
When the rose is opened, then and only then,
will you see it, feel it, and finally know it."

— John Holland

Introduction

The power of the human mind and spirit has always fascinated and amazed me. As a boy, I was the one who saw things differently; I was the one who felt and heard things that others didn't seem to notice; and I was the one whom no one really understood. From an early age, I took it upon myself to read everything I could on metaphysics, spirituality, and psychic phenomena. Instead of playing baseball with my brothers, I'd curl up with a book, trying to figure out why I had these abilities and what to do about them. As I slipped into adulthood, I began to realize that I wasn't that different after all—in fact, there were others like me! Some chose to speak up, while others tried to hide it and push it away in a vain attempt to be "normal." But being psychic or intuitive *is* normal—it's something we're all born with to assist us while we're here on this planet. (I sometimes joke that I don't think God would let us come here without a little help.) Our spiritual abilities are what keep us connected to the Divine.

☒ ☒ ☒

Since the publication and success of my first book, *Born Knowing,* in 2003, I've met thousands of people from all over the world. While many are interested in receiving messages from their loved ones on the Other Side, there are just as many who want to know how they can develop their own psychic and intuitive abilities.

Well, these skills can be harnessed and trained. They can become an unlimited resource for wisdom and guidance, which will greatly assist you in navigating your way through life. Developing your intuitive abilities only takes a commitment to yourself—a commitment to understanding and learning how to live in partnership with your own inner guidance.

To teach what I know, what I believe in, and what I feel passionate about is one of the most fulfilling parts of my life. I've spent more than 20 years developing my own psychic abilities, and I've taught myself to approach the gifts from a more logical, scientific standpoint. As I often say, "If I can't explain it, then what chance do you have?" So this book is meant to be one of education, for within its pages lies the foundation for psychic development and heightened awareness.

In all my studies, and in my own psychic development, one thing has always been clear: You must understand the mechanics of your awareness before you commence your journey. So in this book I'm going to teach you the mechanics of psychic awareness, the benefits of meditation, the vital power of breath, and the workings and functions of your chakras and aura. I'll also teach you how to understand and develop your own *individual* psychic strength. In other words, I hope to empower you to take the first step on your psychic path.

The book you're holding also comes with a meditation CD, which I recommend you use when you've finished the book. I've also included many affirmations throughout *Psychic Navigator,* which will enhance and reinforce each chapter, since they're powerful tools for transformation and self-empowerment. You'll find them at the end of each section—at which point, you may want to take a few moments to stop and repeat them several times so that they become imprinted in your subconscious. Using these affirmations will take you on an experiential journey that will allow you to reinforce and enhance the lessons that you've just learned, or the exercise that you've just carried out. In addition, I've included a few extracts from *Born Knowing* to assist in these teachings.

Throughout this book, I will encourage you to let go of the limitations that have been imposed upon you with respect to the way you think and react. These exercises, meditations, and affirmations are tools that will help you harness your inner guidance. My style of teaching is certainly not the only way, but it has worked for me and my students. I encourage you to read, reach out, and understand even more. You may be attracted to a certain subject that will open a window or door that was closed before, or something may resonate with you that will inspire you to pursue that subject even further. Whatever the case, I congratulate you on searching for what feels right for you.

I hope to instill a sense of openness in you, so you'll become more emotionally and intuitively accepting of the fact that we're indeed more than physical beings—we're also spiritual beings with limitless potential. So take your time to read through *Psychic Navigator,* and then refer to it when you need information or guidance. And always remember: Knowledge takes time, but from it comes wisdom.

Your Never-Ending Guidance

At one time or another, almost everyone has had some kind of psychic experience. Yes, it's true that some people have more extrasensory ability than others, yet we're *all* born psychic. This natural soul power isn't purely limited to transcended masters, or to individuals who have devoted a lifetime to studying and practicing meditation. To be psychic isn't about fortune-telling, crystal balls, or predicting the future; it isn't just something we possess—it's more a way of being.

What Does _Psychic_ Mean?

Put simply, the word _psychic_ is from the Greek word _psychikos,_ meaning "of the soul." By definition, this means that as spiritual beings, we're able to access, receive, and transmit information that reaches beyond our physical body and our natural five senses.

Throughout history, cultures all over the world have honored their spiritual principles and maintained a deep belief that human beings consist of much more than just physical bodies. Traditions were created with rituals (such as chanting, dancing, and meditation) that are still used to this day to remain connected to Spirit and to fully utilize spiritual abilities. Yet psychic abilities aren't exclusive to any particular group: The North American Indians have always had a strong belief in the afterlife and their own soul powers; Aborigines have been known to possess heightened telepathic strengths, which enable them to communicate telepathically with each other over many miles; and in the East, children are educated from an early age about the spiritual energy systems of the human body and its centers.

As I mentioned previously, each and every one of us is equipped with a complex and highly tuned inner guidance system, which we can regularly tap in to by using our extrasensory abilities. Receiving psychic information is all about *energy*. Everything is made up of energy—people, places, and even objects store it. And since we too are energy, we can receive and read information via our psychic senses. Being psychic is similar to the way a television works: We can't see TV signals through the airways because they vibrate at such a high frequency, yet we know they're being transmitted. Our television sets then receive these signals, and they're "descrambled" to form a picture on our screens. Psychic energy works in much the same way—we constantly receive information through our intuition, and the result is an impression or feeling that we didn't receive via our physical senses. As we develop our psychic strengths, we become more proficient at the descrambling.

At this point, I'd like you to take a short break and answer these basic questions:

- Have you ever thought of someone out of the blue, only to run into that person later in the day?

- Can you feel people's moods even before you meet them?

- Have you ever had a hunch that you didn't follow, and later regretted it because it was correct?

- Have you ever known the outcome of a situation or an event before it happens?

- Can you walk into a room and instantly tell what the atmosphere is like?

- Do coincidences and synchronicities keep occurring in your life?

If you answered yes to any of these questions, then it's important to realize that these are just a few examples of what being intuitive or psychic is all about. In other words, it's a sense of *inner awareness*. Being psychic is quite natural and can be a wonderful source of information to help you in life.

One of the most common questions I'm asked is, "Why would I want to develop my psychic or intuitive ability?" I usually respond by asking a set of questions back, such as: "But, wouldn't you like to . . .

. . . improve your relationships?

. . . heighten your creative ability?

. . . help make the most of your career?

. . . receive intuitive guidance on important decisions?

. . . become familiar once again with your spirit?

. . . be connected to your loved ones who have passed on?

. . . enhance your physical abilities?

. . . feel even more connected to nature and the universe?"

You can benefit from all of the above and more by using and strengthening your psychic abilities; however, the one aspect most people have an issue with is trust. Have faith in yourself that you're entitled to live psychically, to see yourself and the world in a way you never thought possible, and let yourself experiment and play like a child when it comes to your abilities. After all, we were all born with a wonderful capacity to play . . . I just encourage you to remember how to do so.

In the following chapters, I'm going to teach you to not only become aware of your inner guidance and the mechanics of how it functions, but I'll also show how you can access it anytime you wish. By doing so, I believe that you'll feel like a complete person. After all, your psychic abilities *are* part of you, so why not use every part of yourself? Once you learn to tap in to the wealth of information you already have, it could very well transform your life!

Affirmations:

"I am opening myself up to my natural intuitive abilities."

"To be truly alive is to be psychic."

Psychic Abilities and Intuition

When my students start exploring their psychic potential, they often ask, "What's the difference between having psychic abilities and intuition?" The words *psychic* and *intuition* are used interchangeably, and there's a fine line between the two. The use of one can often lead to the other, as a natural progression—in fact, psychic abilities are simply the natural extension of our intuition.

You're probably pretty familiar with intuition, which is what causes you to say, "I've got a hunch that . . ." or "My instincts are telling me to . . ." or "I have a gut feeling that . . ." Intuition is that gentle nudge that every so often just comes out of the blue. However, when you learn to *recognize, notice,* and *act upon* these feelings, you'll establish a strong foundation for the development of your psychic abilities. Thus, you'll be able to take control of your intuition, making it work *for* you.

Practicing and using your intuition will result in a stronger link to your psychic awareness, but you may not know where to start or even what tools to use. Before we start, there's one important action I want you to take: Give yourself permission to explore and develop your intuition.

You see, your imagination plays an important part in your intuitive mind. I'm sure you know how easy it is to dismiss an intuitive thought or feeling, as though it was just your mind playing tricks on you. Children are particularly prone to announcing that their imaginary friend is around, or that they're feeling uneasy about someone. It's our adult response to tell kids that it's all in their minds—it's just their imagination. The children then go on to believe that they were wrong, and this is where the seeds of doubt start to grow regarding intuition.

As adults, we regularly dismiss our own insights by telling ourselves that we're imagining things. Yet I believe that a well-developed imagination is a healthy part of the development process, and it can form a bridge between our intuition and our often-dormant psychic abilities.

I've found the following exercise, which I use in my workshops, to be very helpful and fun to do. I'll ask someone to pretend that she's already psychically aware. She will then choose someone else in the room to whom she feels naturally drawn. She's instructed to give any information she's receiving, even if she feels that she's making it up. There's no pressure to be right, so she loosens up and has fun doing it! Her imagination and psychic abilities work hand in hand to create a flow of information. Sure, there are as many misses as there are hits, but the student and the rest of the class become pleasantly surprised at how much accurate information will be given. This is all because they're letting their imagination run free. So it's important to have fun with your imagination as you learn to expand and use your intuition in your daily life—eventually, you *will* tap in to even more of your psychic potential.

Here are some simple suggestions you can try as part of your development:

- Ask yourself, "How many e-mails will I receive this morning?" or "What will my boss be wearing today?"

- When the phone rings, see if you can guess who's on the other end before you pick it up.

- When your utility bill arrives, try to guess how much it is before you open it.

- If you're feeling confident, see if you can divine a word or two from the next day's newspaper headlines.

You can practice these exercises, but also try to make up your own. You may want to write down your experiences in your psychic journal, which we'll discuss later in the chapter. No matter what you decide, keep in mind that you have to *use* your abilities to awaken them, and you need to allow them to guide you. After all, we have everything we need to find the answers right inside our intuitive, psychic selves.

Affirmations:

"I trust the potential of my imagination."
"I have faith in myself and my psychic abilities."

The Importance of Learning the Equipment

Did you know that you're already equipped with one of the fundamental pieces of equipment to provide you with an endless supply of psychic information and guidance? It's your body! It really is this simple: You need look no further than your own physical body for answers.

I got my first real lesson in listening to my body when I was involved in a near-fatal automobile accident, which I described in my first book, *Born Knowing.* The shock to my system due to the accident resulted in my energy centers, which are better known as *chakras* (explained in Chapter 6), being forced open. I soon realized that my abilities, which I'd so often pushed away, were back with a strength and intensity that I'd never experienced before. I still didn't want to just accept this ability without some clear framework of understanding and appreciation—I wanted to know how and why this was happening, and more important, could I control it? After the accident, I devoted myself to studying the vital energies in and around the body. As I said in the previous section, we receive information constantly via our psychic senses, but most people don't realize that their body acts as a conduit in this process. In fact, I liken the body to one big "psychic antenna." However, you don't have to look outside yourself—or get into an accident—to be psychic.

Before you embark on your journey to discover and harness your inner guidance, you should first recognize and accept that you have a psychic spiritual body (as well as a physical body) that operates on its own level of receptivity. For every physical sense you have, there's a psychic sense to complement it; in fact, much research has been carried out to investigate how organs and glands play a vital role in accessing psychic information. These parts of the body don't just work on a physiological level, but they also act as receptors for information outside the physical world, thus helping to access and receive psychic information. Some of these glands and organs include the pituitary and pineal glands, the heart, the nerve endings, the brain, and the stomach. Basically, the *entire* body is used in this process.

Since everything is made of energy, it's important to value this precious commodity and to appreciate its effect on your total physical well-being. Ancient Eastern and Western spiritual philosophies concentrate heavily on the universal life force that runs through everything, including our very selves. This spiritual energy breathes life into our bodies and keeps us connected to the Universal Force that surrounds us all. Chinese medicine calls it *chi,* while the Hindus know it as *prana.* This force surges through our vital organs, permeating our bones, bloodstream, and other parts of the body along a network of internal systems called *meridians.* This spiritual energy is what healers and other natural-health practitioners (such as acupuncturists and massage therapists) work with in the process of removing blockages in our energy system. When ignored, these blockages can manifest themselves in the body as ailments, aches, and pains; or they can create imbalances in our mental and emotional states. Keeping the energy flowing smoothly throughout our system promotes a healthier mind and body. Since we live in a world that's so affected by stress, it's really important to relieve ourselves of it, whether it's through massage therapy, yoga, meditation, or physical exercise. Find out what works best for *you.*

Your body has a way of sending you signals through its own psychic language. Be it a gut response, a physical sensation, an emotion, or even a dream, your body is talking to you! Most of us don't pay enough attention to these impulses or heed such signals until something goes wrong. So during the process of development, don't push those physical sensations or your feelings away. Embrace them and listen to them. Through meditation, you'll often be able to find the answer to what your body is trying to say . . . so just ask. You may not get anything at first, but it's worth persevering, as it really does get easier with practice. To ignore your body and your feelings is to ignore your intuition. For example, I know from experience that when I dream that I'm immersed in water up to my chest, it's often symptomatic of the onset of bronchitis, so I rest and dose up with vitamin C as a precaution. In other words, I *acknowledge* and *act* on the warning signs.

Emily, a young woman who participated in one of my workshops, also successfully listened to her inner voice. She told us that she'd been feeling restless at her high-tech job, so she decided to move on. Emily started going on interviews, and it wasn't long before she was offered a job with a new company—right before the now-famous dot-com crash. The company wanted her to leave her present job immediately, and even though the new position seemed just right for her, Emily noticed that her stomach felt uneasy every time she left their office. Although everything appeared perfect, something just felt wrong. It was as though her gut was trying to tell her, "Something isn't right!" Finally, she trusted her intuition and declined the position. It was the right choice. Two months later Emily found out that the company had been one of those rapid start-ups that was still waiting on round-two funding. It never came, and the company collapsed. But because she *paused, listened to,* and *trusted* her feelings, it saved her from losing a stable job. And there's a happy ending, as

Emily now works for a new company. To this day, she always trusts and uses her abilities when making decisions. So the moral of this story is clear and simple: Listen to what your intuition is telling you.

☒ ☒ ☒

In addition to listening to your inner voice, taking care of your body and your health should be a top priority, especially when you're developing your psychic abilities. Ultimately, *you* are responsible for your physical health. I believe that it's essential to follow a sensible regime of good health, one of balance and moderation: Eat a balanced diet; drink plenty of water; rest; and exercise. If you have a clean and healthy body, you stand a better chance of reducing "blocks," which will greatly help you in becoming more receptive.

Remember that doing psychic work can make you extra sensitive, so you may occasionally feel tired. Mother Nature is a wonderful healer, so try to go for long walks in the woods or at the beach. (And be sure to *breathe!*) When working with your intuitive abilities, it's perfectly okay if it gets to be too much—just take a break from your training for a few days or however long you need. You are *here* in the physical world, and you have to stay balanced and grounded with your physical life as well as your spiritual life.

Your body isn't just a vehicle to get you around while you're here on Earth; it's meant to assist you while your spirit is living in it. Hopefully you'll never look at your body in the same way again. Know how special you *and* your body are—and honor your equipment.

Affirmations:

"Every day and in every way I become stronger and healthier."

"I acknowledge and act upon my body's messages."

Preparing Yourself to Begin

Congratulations on making the decision to become even more of who you really are, and for taking the first steps to discover that you're truly more than this physical body! Now that I've established some of the basics, let's explore and discover your full potential.

Everyone will develop psychically in their own way, in their own time. *Do not rush.* Take all the time you need—after all, it took you many years to pull away from your natural intuitive abilities, so finding your way back isn't going to happen overnight.

First of all, find a room that you can set aside just for you, where you can meditate, study, and practice all the different exercises in this book. If you don't have enough space for a room of your own, try to set aside a corner of another room, or anyplace that can be just yours during your development practice. Most of all, this should be a place where you won't be disturbed when you need to retreat for your quiet time. Shut off the computer, unplug the phone, and know that the e-mail will wait.

Try to make this special place uncluttered; it will also help to be in a well-ventilated area or have a window nearby so that you can let in fresh air to renew the energy. You don't need a lot of furniture—a comfortable chair and a small table are really all that's required. You might want to put fresh flowers in your space to help with the energy; and you may also decide to set up a personal altar with your favorite photos, crystals, and so forth. Some people choose low lighting, burn a votive candle or incense, and play soft music—these aren't necessities, just suggestions. (In my meditation room, I have a comfortable chair, two or three beautiful drawings of my guides for inspiration, and some depictions of spiritual leaders whom I feel connected to. The room is painted in soft blues to create a tranquil atmosphere.) By creating your *own* special area, and only using it for your quiet time, meditation, and personal development, you'll slowly start to infuse the area with positive psychic energy, and it will take on its own feeling. The bottom line is that it should be your very own place of warmth and peace.

⊠ ⊠ ⊠

I find that it's best to meditate and practice at the same time every day so that you can look forward to your special time with yourself and Spirit. By doing so, you'll train your mind and make a commitment, and through regular practice, it will get steadily easier to meditate and develop your inner guidance.

Earlier I stressed the importance of keeping a journal during your development—I highly recommend that you keep it nearby in your special area. You may decide to have more than one in different locations so that no matter where you are, you'll have a place to record your progress, along with those intuitive flashes and impressions. (Remember, psychic thoughts can happen anytime, anywhere.) Your journal will become a valuable resource in the future as you look back on your progress. It will show you where you were right or wrong, and it may even become a teaching manual in itself. I have journals that go back years, in which I recorded hunches, impressions, exercises, and of course, my dreams at night. When I look at them today, I can see the progression of my abilities—in fact, some of my teachings for this book came right from those very journals. But please don't get hung up on whether you were right or wrong—making the effort is the important part, and it will have great value as you discover how your intuition receives information. Once again, it's important to remember that everyone receives and works with their intuitive psychic abilities in their own way, so you should never try to emulate someone else.

As you start your first journal, make sure that you record your entries with a time and date so that you can see your progress when you look back days, months, and years later. Here are a few ideas that you may want to put in your psychic journal:

- Any unexpected thoughts or impressions that come to you that seem to be outside of your day-to-day routine—even if you feel that you're making them up.

- Coincidences and synchronicities that seem to continually run through your life.

- The same numbers that keep showing up in your life, whether you see them on license plates, clocks, phone numbers, or what have you.

- Your dreams, or any images and emotions you remember from your sleep.

- Any pictures or symbols that come into your mind (try not to edit what you're receiving).

- Your personal goals and desires.

- Affirmations that really inspire you (or make up your own).

Just the process of setting up your special area and keeping a psychic journal will by itself help your consciousness expand because you're beginning to make an effort in working with, and getting to know, your own inner guidance system. This will lead to a gradual awakening as you start to notice how you're working together with your mind and spirit in trusting and interpreting the language of your soul.

Enjoy the journey!

Affirmations:

"I give myself permission to visit my sacred space as often as I wish."

"I choose to make a commitment to myself and my inner guidance at this time."

CHAPTER

Discovering Your Psychic Strengths

When we were kids, we were quite psychically aware, but as we grew up, our minds were filled with external influences, from teachers to parents and, of course, the media. Consequently, the intuitive right side of our brain got used less and less, as the left (more analytical) side started to take over.

The result is that as adults we tend to no longer look to our intuition for guidance—instead, we now rely more on our physical senses to make decisions because we've learned to rationalize.

Fortunately, we all possess our own individual "special gifts" and talents—just as some of us are artists, teachers, construction workers, administrative assistants, or what have you, the same can be said for our psychic abilities. We each receive information in different ways, depending on our specific psychic strength. In fact, after studying psychic awareness for many years, I've learned that *everyone* has one or more psychic gift. In this chapter, I'll focus on the three most common: *clairsentience, clairvoyance,* and *clairaudience*. Each ability corresponds to a particular area in the physical body where psychic energy and vibrations are received and identified. (I'll expand on this further in later chapters.)

It's quite natural that some of you will be more proficient in one area over another. If you think that your individual psychic aptitude is to become a "feeler," for example, then you should work to strengthen that skill before you try to move on to developing the other psychic senses. I've noticed that many students who participate in my workshops believe at first that seeing is the best way to receive psychic information, but being a good feeler can also produce excellent results. With time, practice, and patience, you'll be able to use all three of these primary psychic senses so that they work in unison. But as you're starting out, I want you to discover and work with *your* strengths, which is the best way to begin building a solid foundation with your own individual psychic self.

Now let's explore and understand the workings of these abilities, and discover which one (or more) you possess.

Clairsentience

Clairsentience (or "clear feeling") is the inner sense of knowing. It's one of the more familiar psychic strengths, and relatively easy to develop and access. Have you ever walked into a room where an argument recently took place, and you just felt it? When energy lingers on, you end up sensing the emotions that led to that argument through your clairsentient ability. In other words, you *feel* the turbulent, negative energy of that recent altercation.

Here's another example: Let's say you're introduced to someone for the first time, and you immediately get an uneasy feeling. You just *know* you're not really going to bond with that person. What's actually happening is that you're receiving thoughts and feelings from that person's aura that are then transmitted through your abdominal area, resulting in what we so often call a "gut feeling," which is a form of clairsentience.

Indicators of Being Clairsentient

- Are your feelings hurt easily?

- When sitting in a room, can you feel if the furniture isn't positioned right for the room's energy?

- When meeting others, do you intuitively know that something is wrong, even though they appear happy?

- When you're driving, do you sense when you should take a different street than normal, only to find out later that there was a terrible traffic jam on your original route?

- Are you the person everyone goes to when they're feeling down or when they need to get something off their chest?

These are all potential signs of a clairsentient's sensitivity. Many people who are feelers will also receive other people's "stuff," or information outside of themselves. If your natural psychic inclination is to feel, it's also quite probable that you'll pick up vibrations from other people, which will have an effect on your own outlook. I'd like to make a cautionary note here: If you're usually an upbeat kind of person, and for some reason you start feeling down even though there's nothing happening around you to cause this, try approaching it from a different angle. Instead of asking yourself, *"What's* wrong with me?" try asking, *"Who's* wrong with me?"

You see, you may actually be tuning in to the feelings or vibrations from someone else without even knowing it. But your psychic abilities want to help you, so the next time this happens, stop for a few minutes, focus on your solar-plexus area, and ask yourself, "Whose feelings are these?" As you do so, see if an image of someone comes to mind. It could be anyone: a friend, a neighbor, a co-worker, or even your mom. Try calling them to ask how they are—you may be surprised to find out that he or she is the one feeling down. If you're clairsentient, you'll just naturally pick up other peoples' emotions.

We live in a society that's less prone to hugging, touching, or embracing each other—but clairsentients need to touch and feel things physically. The hands are wonderful receptors of energy, so the next time you meet someone new, look into their eyes, reach out and shake their hand, and make a *real* connection. And when you meet a friend, give them a big hug. Just being aware of your clairsentience and the subtle ways you receive information will help you in so many ways, and will also provide a wonderful tool to help find the answers to those unanswered questions.

Exercise

When you're about to make an important decision, whether it has to do with a new relationship, buying a car or a home, or making a business decision, focus on your clairsentient conduit (your solar plexus) and try the following exercise.

First, find somewhere quiet and comfortable to sit. Close your eyes and hold your hands over your solar-plexus area. Imagine that this area of your body is slowly filling up with beautiful yellow light. When you feel settled and comfortable, ask yourself, "How do I feel about this decision?" or "How do I feel about this person?" See if a feeling or an image comes to mind. Next ask, "Does it feel positive or negative?" If you feel uneasy about what you're feeling, then ask again, "Why am I uneasy?" The more specific the questions, the more specific the answers should be.

Now that you have some idea about clairsentience and know how to access this area, experiment in any area of your life you wish. This ability can become highly tuned, or if necessary, you can turn it down to decrease your psychic sensitivity. Just focus on your solar plexus and imagine the yellow light getting smaller. Once you've practiced working with your clairsentience, try going for walks in the country, and open yourself up to feel the outdoors and all its beauty. Since everything is made up of energy, you'll quickly learn to feel it all.

Affirmations:

"I am beginning to develop my clairsentient ability."

*"I safely receive and feel only
what is best for me, as well as others."*

Clairvoyance

Clairvoyance (or "clear seeing") means that your psychic messages are received via images, pictures, symbols, and colors. It's not about seeing in the physical sense with your eyes; rather, it's about using your *inner* eye, which is better known as "the third eye."

Many psychics and mediums "see" in this way. Sometimes you may notice one of them looking away when they're giving a reading—for example, I often look over the left shoulder of my client when I link with those who have passed on. It's not that I'm being rude; it's more that I'm looking at a blank screen with my third eye, which I refer to as my "psychic screen." It's almost as if a mini-movie is playing out right in front of me.

Sometimes the images can be very fleeting or subtle,

which is why most people don't even notice them. Many people also think that some sort of other dimension is going to open up right in front of them with a clairvoyant image. In reality, clairvoyance is more about receiving images, words, or symbols that have their own unique interpretation for each and every one of us. Through time and practice, the same symbols will repeatedly come back to you, and you'll learn how to interpret them by drawing your own analogies. It's important to make a note of these symbols in your journal and see if they feel right to you. They'll become your own "psychic dictionary" for interpreting clairvoyant information.

Indicators of Being Clairvoyant

- Do you often experience vivid, highly memorable dreams?

- Are you the sort of person who doesn't wear a watch because you have the ability to actually visualize what time it is?

- Are you good at picturing exactly where to place furniture to enhance the energy or design of your home or office?

- Have you ever looked at others and known that they were coming down with something, even though they appeared quite healthy?

- When talking to people on the phone, can you envision what they might look like, even though you've never met them before?

If you answered yes to any of these questions, then you could already possess some clairvoyant ability. Don't let popular misconceptions hinder your personal development: Some people can find the unknown a little scary, and the word *clairvoyant* itself can act as a deterrent. People have become influenced by TV shows that often portray clairvoyants with those cliché-ridden images, such as smoke-filled rooms, turbans, and crystal balls. I think it's time to dispel those myths.

Clairvoyance is just seeing through your mind's eye. To be a little more scientific, the reception area for this ability is situated between your brows (the third-eye chakra), and it's associated with the pituitary gland. People who demonstrate a strong tendency toward being clairvoyant often want to spend time in big, open, well-lit spaces. Equally, when they travel, they're the ones who have to see it all—they never want to miss anything! As with clairsentience, once you know how to access the specific reception area and interpret your own symbols and images, the benefits of using your clairvoyant ability can help you as well as others.

Some years ago, I gave a private reading to a woman named Beth. She'd barely walked in when I immediately saw a brand-new computer on her desk in my mind's eye. On the screen, I saw a big red X. Before she even sat down, I launched right in and asked her if she'd recently purchased a computer. She said that she was actually going to look at one after she finished with our reading. From years of practice and my personal symbol directory, I knew what that red X symbol represented—so I advised Beth to have a professional technician look at the machine before she did anything else. A few days later, Beth told me that a friend of hers had thoroughly checked out the computer she was interested in—only to discover that it had been constructed from numerous used parts and wouldn't have lasted more than six months.

A great way to train and sharpen this ability is to listen to visualization tapes that take you on beautiful journeys in your mind's eye. I also recommend that whenever you spend time outside, you try to notice everything around you, whether it's the royal blue sky; the rich, green grass and trees; or the cottony appearance of the clouds. Also, try to notice all the diverse kinds of people you come into contact with each and every day. If you want to immediately see with your psychic eye, then start by really looking at and noticing your surroundings, right here in the physical world. By doing so, you'll be training your eyes and your mind to notice more, which will assist you in developing your clairvoyant strength.

Try the following exercise to understand where your psychic eye is and to help expand your psychic vision.

Exercise

Again, as with all the exercises in this book, find a quiet, comfortable place where you're not going to be disturbed. Get a small white votive candle and sit comfortably with the candle in front of you. Relax your eyes and stare into the flame. You'll feel your eyes start to water; when they do, close them and put the palm of each hand over each eye to create a total blackout. You should now start to notice that the flame is flickering slightly above and between your brows. Wait until the flame disappears, then do the exercise again for another 10 to 15 minutes. What you're actually doing is training and developing your clairvoyant eye. So now you know that this special spot is just above the bridge of your nose, *not* where you look straight out with your physical vision.

The next time you want to use your psychic abilities to help answer a question or a decision, start by closing your eyes and gently focusing on your third-eye area, then go ahead and ask the question. (As always, remember to be specific.) When you've done so, write down in your journal whether you saw a symbol, a word, a color, a person, or even an object. By practicing and experimenting, you'll continue to sharpen this ability.

Start off small with some simple tests—for example, try to guess the suit of playing cards after turning them upside down. I used to play the following game with my mother when I was a child (little did I know that I was training my young psychic abilities!). Have a friend think of number from 1 to 50 and see if you can visualize it. Go with the first answer that pops into your psychic vision. Another great experiment is to have someone stand in another room and choose something to hold in their hands. Keep a mental note of what you see, whether it's an image or an outline. Trust what you're receiving before your logical mind tries to shoot it down. These exercises may seem elementary, but what's actually happening is that you're beginning to stretch your abilities once again. Remember the saying "Use it or lose it"!

You can also make up your own experiments—there's so much more to see once you learn to use this remarkable ability!

Affirmations:

"I am beginning to develop my clairvoyant ability."

"More and more, I notice all the beauty around me."

Clairaudience

Clairaudience, or the inner sense of hearing, is the ability to hear names, dates, certain sayings, and yes, even songs and melodies. When you hear *subjectively* (that is, in your mind), you'll become aware of sounds as though they're words spoken in your own voice. This is why clairaudience can be a little confusing when determining if these are your own, or psychic, thoughts. With practice, you'll be able to differentiate between the two.

It's also important to point out that some people hear *objectively,* which is outside themselves. For instance, have you ever heard your name called out, only to find that no one was there? It may be from a loved one in Spirit, or it can be someone here who may be thinking of you. If you feel it's the latter, try calling that person to say hi. They'll probably tell you that they were just thinking of you.

Another good example of clairaudience is when you hear a song playing in your head. Stop for a minute and make a mental note of what the song is; then when you have a chance, listen to the words. All too often, there will be a message of encouragement or advice for you or for someone close to you who needs a little lift. This ability can be accessed through the throat-reception area (throat chakra), and clairaudients can increase their psychic listening strength by focusing on this area.

Indicators of Being Clairaudient

- Do you always think inside your head instead of out loud?

- Can you tell when someone isn't telling the truth?

- Are you attracted to loud places?

- Do you usually have music playing in the background no matter what you're doing?

- Do you ever hear what others are thinking?

If you answered yes to any of these questions, then you probably pay great attention to that still small voice that you so often hear. You know, the one that so many of us don't listen to enough, only to regret it later. . . .

The first stage of developing your clairaudient ability must begin by differentiating psychic information from your everyday thoughts and mind chatter. To do this, you'll need to practice improving your clairaudience. Over time, the information you receive via your inner voice will start to flow and will develop a sharper sense of clarity. Generally, this information should have a positive tone to it. If you're receiving negative information, then it's likely that some degree of interference is coming from your own mind. In this instance, you should consider checking to see if there are emotional or psychological issues that need addressing before you continue.

One very important piece of information I give to people who are beginning their psychic training is this: When you believe that you're receiving psychic information, step back and ask yourself, "Is this information coming *to* me or *from* me?" By doing so, you'll remain subjective at all times.

As you develop further, you'll be able to access your psychic hearing to assist you in many areas of your life. If clairaudience is your strength, then try the following exercises.

Exercise

This time, find a comfortable place outdoors, such as a park or at the beach, but somewhere that people of all ages come together. Close your eyes, and breathe in slowly and relax. Now, just *listen* with your physical hearing. Try to focus on the sounds from far off in the distance—can you can hear the traffic, the birds chirping, or airplanes flying overhead? Reach out as far as you can with your hearing, and slowly bring your awareness closer to your surroundings. Can you hear the children playing? Can you hear what other people are saying? Try to figure out the age difference in their voices. Are they young or old? Are there animals in the area? Notice all sounds far and near at the same time. Now, while this is happening, try to listen to the silence in between the sounds, which is the special place where the undercurrent of psychic information can often be heard.

This exercise trains your physical hearing to reach different levels and ranges. By doing so, you'll actually sharpen your clairaudience, as well as listening outside of yourself. The best advice I can give you now is this: Begin to *really* listen.

Exercise

Sit or lie down in a comfortable, quiet position in your special room or area. Take a deep breath, close your eyes, and let the day slip away. Now imagine that there's a beautiful sky-blue light situated in your throat area. Imagine that this light is slowly expanding as you breathe into the center of your throat (where clairaudience is accessed). Take a few moments to ask any question that you'd like information or guidance on, but as you're asking, keep your awareness in this area and on the sky-blue light. If at first you don't hear anything, don't be put off.

You may receive a word or even a sentence—does the answer you receive relate to the question you asked? If you don't understand the answer, ask yourself what it means to you. More information could flow, or your inner guidance may want to stick to the answer it originally gave you. Trust what you're receiving, for you may notice at a later date or time that it was the perfect answer. And the next time you go into a meeting, take a few moments to focus on your throat area and ask, "What do I need to know for this meeting?" A word of advice may come to you, or even a song or symbol that somehow seems to speak to you in its own way.

Your angels and guides are also waiting to assist you. All you have to do is ask them a question and listen for their guidance. Make a note in your journal of what you're receiving and date it—the information might not make sense now, but it probably will later on. As I've said before, don't forget to ask, "Is this coming *to* me or *from* me?"

Affirmations:

"I am beginning to develop my clairaudient ability."

"More and more, I notice all the sounds around me."

⊠ ⊠ ⊠

As you learn to reawaken and develop your individual psychic abilities—whether it's clairsentience, clairvoyance, or clairaudience—please remember to stay grounded and balanced. When these abilities are properly developed, they can greatly assist you in *all* areas of your life, but most important, they'll benefit your spiritual development. It should be a wonderful experience as you discover and build up your psychic strength. And flex those intuitive muscles! After all, the more you use them, the stronger they'll get. It really is that simple.

⊠ ⊠ ⊠ ⊠

CHAPTER

Into the Stillness

For many people, meditation conjures up images of a guru chanting from the top of a mountain, or a monk sitting in quiet solitude in a sacred temple, surrounded by incense smoke floating in the air. Others believe that this practice is as simple as closing your eyes and going into a trance; or at the most basic level, you only need to let your mind go totally blank to enter some type of meditative state. In this chapter, we'll take a closer look at this ancient method of meditation, stillness, and guidance.

What Is Meditation?

Meditation is merely a state of being, in which your active mind slows down. It can bring you to a place where you silence your mental chatter, and in doing so, you become increasingly aware of the subtle, shifting energies within you. It may seem impossible, but you can actually train yourself to watch your thoughts come into your mind and go right out again, much like flowing water. Soon these same thoughts will lose their power to influence your conscious mind.

To develop your psychic/intuitive guidance system, it's essential that you learn to enter and feel comfortable with the silence within—meditation is a vital part of the process. Now it's fine to read about this practice, but to put it simply, you just have to do it!

It's possible to enter into a state of meditation when you consciously focus your mind on a single point. Some people find that using a *mandala* (those beautiful images of visual symbols that draw you in) is helpful, while others visualize images such as a flower, a beautiful landscape, or their spiritual guide. Still others prefer to continually chant, using a single word or sound. Whatever method you choose, with steady practice and commitment you'll ultimately train your mind to be still, which will foster a sense of well-being that can have tangible benefits in all areas of your life.

If you believe that you can't meditate, you may be surprised to find out that you've already done it without even realizing it. For example, have you ever become so absorbed in something that you've totally lost yourself? Have you ever just "zoned out," or had that sensation of time just slipping by? If so, you've most likely crossed over into a state of meditation.

☒ ☒ ☒

We live in a world where so many of us strive to earn more, get better jobs, and buy newer cars and other material items that we believe we need to feel successful. This is all well and good, but most of us are finding it harder to get fulfillment from the outside material world, so we're starting to look for the answers from within. It's my belief that above all, it's important to continually feed our souls. When we constantly reach outward to achieve more and more, it's easy to slip farther and farther away from our divine force. (Yes, I'm referring to our spirit, which you can call whatever you want.) I find that meditation is a great way for me to *look* at a problem or situation instead of being *in* it. It's a chance to stand back, view the issue through new eyes and with a renewed appreciation, and see where the changes can be made for a healthier or more beneficial outcome.

When the outside world becomes so stressful that your anxiety starts to overwhelm you, stop and ask yourself, "When was the last time I checked in with myself?" You've got to learn to pull back from the stresses and strains of daily life and make time to seek out that inner place of silence, calmness, and peace. Meditation can do all that, but it can also positively affect your health, which I call the "extra benefit." For instance, the sense of relaxation and calmness that results from meditating can enhance your immune system and reduce your blood pressure. It can also increase your physical energy as well as your overall well-being.

Now, here's a reality check. You may have the best intentions to start your meditation practice, but life will throw up lots of hurdles to try to stop you. That's when you have to make an extra effort to devote time to it. To get into the mind-set, I suggest that you start by practicing at the same time every day, whenever you feel is the best time for you. (Personally, I prefer mornings before I start work. By doing so, I approach the day calm, centered, and ready to take on the world with a sense of awareness, clarity, and vitality.)

Even when life tries to pull you away from doing your meditation, keep at it, at least for seven days. Hopefully, once you've settled into a routine, you'll continue the practice for the rest of your life . . . and wonder why you waited for so long. Start with 15 minutes each day, using some of the exercises in this chapter—soon you'll learn to increase the length of your meditation, and ultimately you'll look forward to that special time with yourself and your spirit.

Affirmations:

"I am taking time each day to enter the silence within me."

"Every day and in every way, my inner guidance is enhanced through meditation."

Relaxing the Body and Mind

If you choose to become more aware of your inner guidance system, then you must first learn to relax your body as well as your mind. When your physical state is one of calmness, your mind will become still, and clarity will follow. Meditation will help you integrate your body, mind, and spirit, so you'll feel centered and grounded, which will promote a state of balance. You'll feel more capable of dealing with your busy schedule, and over time you'll alleviate some of the tensions you hold inside your body. Once that stress is released, some associated minor ailments may disappear as well.

The body and the mind are in a state of constant inter-action. The process of *blending* the two, using the art of meditation, will ultimately make it difficult to differentiate between them—in other words, you'll reach a state of one-ness. When you achieve this state, you'll be free to explore more of your spirit and discover a deeper understanding of your true self. You'll discover who you really are, and real-ize that every one of us is connected, and always will be, to the universal energies that are available to help and guide us.

If you've already set up your special meditation room or area, I want to encourage you once again to start medi-tating in it as much as possible, at the same time every day. By doing so, you'll increase the peaceful energy vibrations within and around your space. These will continue to build up over time—so when you walk back in, you'll feel that positive energy, and it will become easier and quicker to enter a state of relaxation.

Exercise

This is a simple exercise to assist you in relaxing your body and to prepare you for meditation. It's designed to help you increase your body awareness, so before we begin, get com-fortable. Make sure that you're wearing loose-fitting, comfort-able clothing to prevent any physical restrictions. Sit comfortably in a straight-backed chair, with your feet flat on the ground and your hands resting on your lap. For this exercise, it's better to sit rather than lie down, as I don't want you to fall asleep. It's important for you to be alert and aware when you're meditating.

Now close your eyes, breathe in slowly, and gently exhale all that tension. Once again, breathe. Gently move all the parts of your body as you settle into a relaxed state. Try to become aware of your left foot—slowly focus your attention there, tensing and relaxing the area. Gradually move your attention up your left leg, taking notice of any tension here. If so, raise your left leg, try tensing the muscles, release them, and relax. Continue breathing, then slowly let your awareness travel up your left side, into your abdominal area, up your chest, to your shoulder, and down your left arm—all the way to your fingers. Clench your left hand into a fist and relax. Move your awareness up your arm again to your shoulder, down your neck, and all the way down your back. Whenever you feel any tension, just tense the muscles, release, relax, and move on. Now slowly move your awareness up to your entire head, scalp, and face, and let go of any tightness in your jaw. Release any tension, and feel the sense of relaxation take over.

Once you've worked up the left side, do the same for the right side—but this time, start from the head. Then move down your right shoulder, arm, hand, thigh, calf, foot, and on to your toes. Once again, let your awareness slowly scan your entire body to see if there's one place that's calling out for attention. Always release the tension and relax.

Notice if there's still any tension in a certain area; if so, tense and gently release. Ask your body if that certain spot is holding on to a past memory or emotion that needs to be released. There's no need to rush here—try to notice which body part needs more attention or effort to relax than another. Take your time and spend a moment with that part of your body, letting the healing relaxation begin to move through this area and on to the rest of the body.

If you're feeling tense, this simple exercise will help you release the stress, and at the same time, it will make it easier for you to practice future meditations.

During these early stages of learning to meditate, you'll notice that your mind will continue to chatter and wander off, allowing external influences to creep in. That's perfectly normal at the beginning. Over time, your mind will slow down, the chatter will diminish, and you'll start to gain a sense of clarity and focus. Once you've learned how to relax and become aware of your body, you'll be ready to move on to the next exercise, which stills your mind. When you're calm and free from internal noise, it will be easier to find that place of absolute stillness where psychic and intuitive information flows freely and easily.

Exercise

Close your eyes, and simply focus on your breath. Take your time. With each breath in, you'll become more relaxed, and with each exhalation, you'll let go of all that stress and tension. Try this for five minutes, focusing on the regular rhythm of your breathing. Let it all go, and relax. If your mind starts to wander, just focus back on your breath. If thoughts come in, acknowledge them, and slowly watch them leave. Notice how it feels to be completely relaxed. Continue to focus on your breath while you let all that mind chatter slow down and evaporate.

In your mind's eye (or your "third eye") located between your eyebrows, I want you to imagine a symbol of your choosing. It can be a flower, a religious figure or icon, a single word, or whatever's pleasing to you. Make it your own special symbol, which you'll use every time you meditate. At this point, just focus without straining on your chosen symbol. Now slowly inhale—but this time, bring your awareness up to your third eye as you focus on your symbol. It's almost as if you're breathing in and out through this center. Do this for another five minutes. If your mind wanders, focus on the breath and your symbol to bring you back.

During this relaxed state, ask your Higher Self for answers to any questions you might have. You may see an image, a scene, or beautiful colors. You can even allow your spirit guides to make themselves known to you. The answers you seek may not be immediate—sometimes they won't even present themselves until a few days later. Yet you may be at the right place at the right time to receive your answers immediately. After about 15 minutes, slowly move your fingers as you bring your awareness back to your body, and start to become aware of the room around you again. Remain seated for a moment and contemplate your meditation, so you can remember how calm you feel now that you've achieved the process of stilling the mind. In this peaceful state, anything is possible!

Meditation is an amazing practice because it's filled with so many wonderful surprises. If you practice before you go to sleep at night, a dream may even provide you with answers. For this reason, it's helpful to keep your journal nearby after your meditation, or beside the bed so it's right there when you wake up in the morning. It's also a good idea to write everything down in your journal when you first open your eyes in the morning, even before your feet touch the floor. Do it before your mind brings you back into a state of full waking consciousness.

Affirmations:

"My body, mind, and spirit are one."
"I am centered, balanced, and calm."

Active Meditation

It's fascinating to watch people work their way through a labyrinth or maze. While some are obviously looking to find their way out, others are often involved in what's known as a "walking meditation," or a form of *meditation in action,* in which the experience of walking is used as a catalyst to combine movement with inner calmness. (You see, anytime you actively focus your mind on a single point or activity with a sense of concentration, you can enter some form of a meditation.) Now the most important point of all active meditations is to be fully aware of the routine activity that you're carrying out. In other words, if you're walking, just walk; if you're running, just run; and if you're washing dishes, just wash the dishes. Every time your mind starts to wander, focus on what you're doing and bring it back to the task at hand.

The walking meditation is a beneficial alternative when sitting meditations are getting too repetitive or when you're looking for a change in your routine. When you practice this form of meditation, you allow yourself to experience and be with the actual sensation of counting your footsteps. Concentrating only on the path before you, your pace slows, your breathing deepens, and your mind becomes clear. As you do this, you'll focus on the present, and with each step, you'll be able to stop yourself from thinking about the past or the future.

Keep in mind that even though you're walking, your mind will still have a tendency to wander, as there is so much visual stimuli outdoors. Initially, it will be challenging to block out all the images around you or the sensory onslaught of sounds and smells from the environment. You may also catch yourself thinking, *I wonder if I have any e-mail. What will the kids want for dinner?* or even *Why am I doing this?* When this happens, always bring your awareness back to the steady rhythm of your step.

You can practice this meditation anytime you wish, but try to find a track or an area that's flat outdoors. (A cleared path in the woods also works beautifully.) Some people prefer to simply walk in a circle, whether it's indoors or outdoors . . . or maybe you'll find your own labyrinth.

Exercise

Begin by simply standing still in one spot. Let yourself feel the weight transferring to the soles of your feet as you connect with the earth below. If the conditions are right, try going barefoot for an even better connection to your active meditation, as well as the earth. Now shift your body from one foot to the other, and begin to notice how your posture feels as you lift up

your head and push your shoulders back as you breathe in. If it would feel more comfortable, let your arms hang naturally or hold your hands lightly together in front of you. Notice what's around you before you begin. Now focus your gaze at a point slightly in front of you on the ground to help you avoid any visual distractions.

Start walking, and with each step, count a number from 1 to 10. Count down from 10 to 1 again, and then start again from 1 up to 10. As you walk and count, keep your focus only on the sole of each foot as it hits the ground, rather than on any other parts of your body. As you count, you're continually bringing your awareness and focus back to the present.

If you lose your count, or you find yourself thinking while you're walking, go back to the counting and start again. After about 15 minutes, come to a natural halt. Take your time so that you're not forced to come to a sudden stop. Feel your soles once again on the earth, and switch your weight from one foot to the other so you just experience standing and being still. Breathe, and enjoy being in the present.

Start off practicing this exercise for 15 minutes, but slowly build up your time. It may seem easy as you read about it, and it doesn't sound like much to accomplish, but let me assure you, it is. If you practice both sitting and walking meditations as well as other active meditations, your awareness and concentration will develop naturally.

You'll soon start to notice the positive impact on all your everyday activities. This is a powerful meditation, and apart from it being enjoyable, it's highly beneficial to your overall psychic training.

Affirmations:

"I live in the present moment."

"My awareness and focus are constantly improving with everything I do."

Accessing Your Higher Mind

The more we stay connected to our Higher Mind—which we also call the Universe, the Source, or *Spirit*—the more we strengthen and build that crucial bridge between ourselves and our higher consciousness. While we're all born connected to this Divine awareness, we have a tendency to pull away from what was once natural. It's reasonable to assume that when we become disconnected from our Higher Mind, the source that once nourished us will be replaced with something else. In other words, the connection could be with food, alcohol, nicotine, codependency to someone or something, or even work. Many of us spend our lives trying to fill that void that was created when the link was broken.

However, it *is* possible to get reacquainted with your Higher Mind again. As you develop the ability to raise yourself above the conscious mind and all its impulses and distractions, you'll find that place of stillness and peace, and possibly some answers. This is the part of yourself that can give you a sense of the bigger picture, where mundane details seem less important. It's also the part of you that wants nothing more than for you to be happy, and to put you on the right path for your psychic and spiritual development. When you face difficult situations in your life, try to remember to consult with your Higher Mind—after all, it's always been there and always will be part of who *you* are.

Many years ago, when I was studying and developing in England, I was fortunate to learn the following technique. My tutors taught me that when we're worried, depressed, unsure of ourselves, or confused, we have a tendency to "think down." How often have we said, "I'm feeling down" or "I can't get out of my own way"? What we're really saying is that our thoughts seem to be trapped inside of us. When this happens, we tend to repeatedly dwell on the same thought, a bit like a broken record. This then leads to stress and worrying, which often results in a sense of confusion. (I know we can all relate to this!) My tutors taught me how to "think up"; that is, even when we're feeling down, to bring our thoughts up and out of our body.

The following exercise will assist you in accessing your Higher Mind and to think up, getting you out of your head. It will also be beneficial during those times when you need a little extra guidance.

Exercise

Make yourself comfortable, close your eyes, and relax. (You may want to try Exercise 1 on page 44 to relax your body before you begin this one.)

Bring your awareness to the bottom of your feet. Let your breath assist you in transferring the relaxing energy up through the bottom of your feet. Slowly work your way up your calves, your thighs, your abdomen, your chest, your fingers, your hands, your arms, your shoulders, your neck, your face . . . right to the top of your head. Now I want you to imagine that there's one big funnel starting to form on top of your head, reaching out into the universe. Think of it as a vortex of energy reaching upward.

Let your awareness constantly flow *up* and *out* of your head and into this funnel above you. All the information you want can be accessed and brought to you. You may want to imagine a shimmering ball or cloud of white light above this funnel. Now reach up with your mind, as if you're floating and blending with this brilliant white light. Slowly merge yourself into this space as you continue to reach up and out of your body with your mind. Take a few moments with this energy, and feel what it's like to be calm and centered, to be one with your Higher Mind.

Now it's time to ask your Higher Mind a question. For example:

- Is there someone you'd like to get along with, but you're not sure how to go about it?

- Is there a question about your job that you need guidance on?

- Are you wondering what's stopping you from reaching your goals?

You can even ask if there's something that your intuition has been trying to tell you. Ask your Higher Mind how you can be more receptive when it's trying to communicate with you. You may want to ask, "What steps can I take to improve my life and spiritual development?" Ask one question at a time, and wait for a response. Take whatever answers come to you—you may receive a symbol, words, or even a feeling. Don't be surprised if your Higher Mind also chooses to make known a certain area of your life that you're neglecting. Sometimes, to paraphrase that old song, you don't always get what you ask for—but you'll get what you need. Remember what you've received so that you can bring the information and answers back into your conscious mind.

It's now time to bring your awareness back into your body. Don't worry—you'll be able to return to the special place you've just discovered anytime you wish. Slowly take a breath and let it assist you in coming back to the present. Feel yourself shifting down into your body, entering through the open funnel. Move your fingers and toes, and gently open your eyes to become fully aware of your body and the room around you.

I often teach this technique in my workshops, but in the early stages of development, I encourage my students to start off by asking small questions at first so that they can familiarize themselves with the meditation and learn to differentiate their conscious thinking from their Higher Minds. So don't worry if you feel as though you didn't get any answers immediately, as you'll probably get them in another way, or a day or two later, or maybe from someone else unexpectedly. Be open to letting your Higher Mind speak to you in various ways. As always, keep your journal at the ready for when you come out of the meditation so that you can take the time to interpret what the words, feelings, and symbols specifically mean for you.

You'll know when your Higher Mind is speaking and answering your questions because you'll feel a sense of smoothness with respect to what you're receiving. The answers *will not* sound like your regular mind chatter. I want to stress again here that any information you may receive from your Higher

Mind should *always* be of a positive nature. Ask yourself the question once again: "Is this coming *to* me or *from* me?"

This meditation can be used anytime you need it— especially during stressful times in your life, when you may need an intuitive solution. Try to get into the habit of shifting up and accessing your Higher Mind at least once a day. With practice, you'll be able to seek insightful guidance anytime you wish. By using the meditations and exercises in this chapter, you'll gain a sense of transformation and inner wisdom that can reach into every aspect of life, and could possibly be the key to opening the door to an old friend: your spirit.

Affirmations:

"I trust my Higher Mind's wisdom."
"My Higher Mind is always there to assist me."

CHAPTER

The Vital Force

We all have a remarkable resource inside of us that can be accessed at any time and is totally free! I have my own special name for it: "the psychic-energy reservoir," and it can benefit you greatly in your overall well-being and help your psychic and intuitive development. And all you have to do to tap in to it is simply—take your next breath!

Breath Awareness

When I started exploring the mechanics of my own psychic abilities, I found myself drawn to Eastern traditions, specifically the value and significance of working with the breath. These traditions are based on the principle that breath *is* life, and it's the bridge between the body and soul. After all, when we enter this world, the first thing we do is inhale—and before we leave this life, the last thing we do is exhale. If you think about it, life is one continuous series of breaths.

Eastern teachers have thankfully passed on their philosophies and techniques to many of us in the West. We've learned that in addition to the physical benefits resulting from proper breathing habits, our mental abilities, happiness, willpower, and spiritual progression will advance by understanding the mechanics of proper breathing. So many of us take this unassuming miracle for granted; however, once the breath becomes part of our everyday awareness, we'll begin to wonder how we could have ever failed to pay attention to it.

Who would believe that we actually need instructions on the proper way to breathe? In this high-tech age, we rarely stop to catch our breath; consequently, we've developed so many unnatural and unhealthy ways of standing, sitting, and even talking that our postures quickly fall out of alignment. This then leads to constrictions in the chest, which prevent us from breathing properly . . . and to half breathe is to be half alive. Basically, the way we breathe is how we live our lives: If we're breathing with shallow, restricted, short breaths, it's more than likely that we're holding on to or suppressing our emotions. Therefore, we're limiting the potential of our lives and our very selves.

To appreciate proper breathing, just watch babies sleeping. Notice how they breathe in and out slowly, with their abdomens rising up and down—of course, we all breathed this way at one time. Today, when you integrate your mind and body with the help of the breath, you can experience a more enlightened, healthy, and positive life experience. You see, through the breath we draw in psychic energy, which is known as *prana,* a Sanskrit word that means "absolute energy."

Prana is the universal principle of energy or force, which can be found in all forms of life. We're constantly breathing in air charged with prana, so by controlling and regulating our breathing, it's possible to acquire more of this valuable psychic energy source. The yogis know that by practicing certain breathing exercises, they can draw on prana to use in every part of their lives, whether it's for meditation, relaxation, or even manifesting a goal; it can also be directed to work on a certain part of the body and assist in a localized healing process.

It may take a little time and practice to work with your breath—or to even become aware of it again—but it will play an important role in how you act, feel, think, and live the rest of your life.

In the following sections, I'll talk more about prana, and we'll practice some techniques for proper breathing, along with breathing meditations. Using breath in your meditations, or just learning to breathe properly for yourself, can be a valuable tool in developing your body-mind connection, as well as your spirit. When you learn to breathe the way you were meant to, and when you begin to feel the vitality and other benefits of working consciously with the breath, you'll be on your way to living a life of unlimited potential!

Affirmations:

"Every day I am becoming more aware of my breath."

"My breath is my own personal healing tool."

The Complete Breath

During my mediumship training in England, I came across a man who practiced the psychic arts that he'd learned from the yogis in the East, including a technique called "The

Complete Breath." To this day, I remember him telling me that "it's important to remember, you *are* your breath."

As I sat there, fascinated, in his classroom, I knew that this philosophy somehow resonated with me. I started working with my breath—and soon realized that it would be an ongoing process, one that would change and evolve, much like turning the pages of a fascinating book. Nevertheless, as I developed, I discovered new things about myself, my emotions, my body, and my thoughts, which revealed a new sense of intimacy with my spirit. I experienced a deeper and more profound sense of self-love.

◹ ◹ ◹

Remember how I suggested that you notice the way a baby breathes? Well, I'd like you to keep in mind that as we get older, most of us only tend to breathe into the upper part of our chest. So, this next exercise deals with three-part breathing, which uses the entire respiratory system. The lower, middle, and upper areas of your lungs are used to expand your chest cavity in all directions, thus incorporating a combination of low, mid, and high breaths. When done properly and in order, the three will flow to their own rhythm to become one continuous Complete Breath.

I urge everyone to learn the Complete Breath technique before going on, as the exercises in the following sections are based on using and working with this particular type of breathing.[1] As much as you may want to skip ahead, this method is the foundation that should be studied and mastered first. (To further your knowledge with respect to the breath, I highly recommend that you read *Science of Breath* by Yogi Ramacharaka.)

The Complete Breath isn't meant to be forced or uncomfortable—instead, I'm trying to encourage you to go back to the way nature meant for you to breathe. Please note that when you do this exercise, you *don't* have to overfill your lungs with every inhalation. You can inhale a normal amount of air, which you'll then learn to distribute evenly to the three parts of your lungs.

Please thoroughly read the following exercise so that you get a good idea of what I'd like you to be able to achieve with this exercise. Once you've done that, you're ready to begin.

---

1. **Note:** The exercises in this chapter are not meant to be forced, and should not result in holding your breath for long periods of time. For the maximum benefit, they should be carried out slowly and with patience; however, if you feel any physical discomfort, please stop immediately and return to your normal style of breathing. You may also want to visit your doctor first to make sure that these exercises aren't too strenuous for your system.

Exercise

Lie down or sit with your back straight, and get nice and comfortable. Breathe through your nostrils, inhaling steadily. Slowly breathe into your stomach, letting the air move up to your lower lungs and then into the chest area. Hold your breath for a few seconds, and then exhale very slowly—hold your chest in a firm position, draw in your abdomen slightly, and slowly lift it upward as the air leaves your lungs. When all the air is exhaled, relax your chest and abdomen.

This exercise should be carried out in one slow, continuous breath, which will be distributed to all three parts of the lungs. Some people prefer to practice it in a mirror while placing their hands on their abdomen, lower ribs, and upper chest. You can also try using a rolled-up blanket placed on the three different areas one at a time, which will help you feel the breath rise and fall in each area. At the beginning, this exercise will seem a little "jerky" as you breathe into the three parts of the lungs. But soon you'll be able to complete this in one smooth breath. Once you've learned to master the Complete Breath, you'll quickly understand how it will benefit you in all your future breath work and meditations. Try to do this exercise a few times a day to help you get into the feeling of breathing freely, calmly, and most important—completely.

Affirmations:

"With every breath, I feel whole and complete."
"I safely use my breath in all areas of my life."

Mindfulness of Breathing

Whenever I can, I spend Tuesday nights in a very special way: I join a small group at a Buddhist temple that's hidden in the woods, where Mother Nature seems to cradle this special place safely within her arms. (Sometimes I prefer to meditate in a group or a spiritual environment because the energy that emanates from the rest of the group seems to really support and enhance the beauty of experiencing oneness.) Here, a monk in his sacred robes slowly walks in, bows to a large golden statue of Buddha, and rings the gong, which resonates throughout the temple dome. This same monk once taught all who gathered about the "Mindfulness of Breathing," which I now practice faithfully. I regularly use it to assist me in my meditations, to relax, to simply fall into a peaceful sleep, or to just stop for a few minutes during the day to take a mental break.

Of course, you don't have to be a Buddhist or even sit with a group to practice this technique, which will help you develop and strengthen the power of mindfulness. This simply means that you'll become aware of the breath as a meditative tool. By observing your breath, you'll be able to enter into a deeper form of relaxation while remaining alert, thus opening up your mind, body, and consciousness to the power of the breath.

Mindfulness is the opposite of distraction—it's the ability to maintain an easy sense of focus and attention, and it's a way to keep your mind from flitting from thought to thought, just by the simple act of mindful breathing. The more mindful you are, the more aware you are of yourself and what's going on inside of you, as well as what's going on outside and beyond yourself.

In the following exercise, you'll be using your breath as an object of focus and attention. There's no need to force concentration by fixing your attention on your breath, or holding it with determination. Try to notice how one breath follows the other without effort. The breath will breathe *you* when you do this exercise—that is, you'll become more attuned to its rhythm, its inward and outward flow, and the sensations and feelings that go with it. Practice this exercise anytime you wish—hopefully, like me, you'll continue to do so for the rest of your life.

Exercise

Make yourself comfortable, preferably sitting with your feet flat on the floor and your hands in your lap. (Note that for this exercise, you'll be using your nose to inhale as well as exhale.) There are four steps included here, and it's important that you complete all four in the right order, as each step will assist you in observing and experiencing your breath.

This breathing meditation can be done for approximately 20 minutes, or you can extend it longer if you wish. It doesn't matter in the beginning how long you take—the main thing is to *just do it.* Remember, each step should take about five minutes.

Close your eyes and relax . . . and let's begin with **Step 1.**

Count your breath to help you connect with it. Just watch it come and go with as little effort as possible, as it follows its own natural rhythm. Count at the *end* of each outgoing breath. Count 10 breaths in the same way. For example: Breathe in, breathe out, and count 1; breathe in, breathe out, and count 2; and so on up to 10. Now count for another 10 breaths: Breathe in, breathe out. It's that simple. Continue for five minutes and move on.

In **Step 2,** I'd like you to change so that you're counting just *before* the incoming breath. Although this change is quite subtle, it will create a different emphasis in the way you focus and pay attention to the breath. For example: Count 1, breathe in, and breathe out; count 2, breathe in, breathe out; and so on up to 10. Continue for 10 breath cycles.

Now for **Step 3,** let go of the counting completely, and simply watch your breath come and go without effort. Enjoy the experience as you become even more aware of the total sensation of breathing. Also pay attention to those small spaces between the breaths.

Finally, for **Step 4,** lightly focus your attention on the feeling near the tip of your nose and lips as your breath comes and goes. Try not to strain or force anything at this point. Just relax and concentrate on your breath.

This particular breathing meditation is a wonderful way to spend some time each day not *doing* anything, but just *being.* The time you spend observing your breath will not only restore you physically, emotionally, and mentally, but it will also instill you with a sense of peace and alignment with your spirit. Your breath has its own way of constantly reminding you to remain in the here-and-now; by working with it, you'll learn to let go of the past, stop worrying about what will be, and ease the stresses and strains of everyday life. You'll start to focus on today, this very moment—after all, that's where the intuitive answers and the true power reside, and where you'll be able to let go and gently relax into the present.

Affirmations:

"My breath and I are one."

"The more I learn to watch my breath, the calmer I become."

Psychic Breathing Techniques

The human body is sustained by the same prana that nourishes the universe. The body (your equipment) has the ability to control and use this special energy through the use of "pranayama." Don't let the word scare you—it just means to *control, channel,* and *direct* the flow of prana through the use of breath.

When your body is depleted of prana, you'll tend to feel tired or unwell—consequently, your breath *must* come first. So, when you start asking yourself, "Why am I looking fatigued, feeling stressed, or just generally out of balance?" stop for a moment and think about how you've been breathing recently. (Of course, a healthy life is more than just breathing.)

Prana is such an essential psychic force that I believe we should all be aware of its existence. You can and will have access to this universal reservoir because no one is excluded—it's there for everyone. Besides learning the proper way to breathe, which helps you physically by bringing more prana into your body, I want to show you how it can also help you on a psychic/spiritual level. Prana enlivens matter and can assist in heightening the vibrations of your chakras and your aura, which in turn will increase your psychic awareness. That's why I've called this section "Psychic Breathing."

Prana can also play a big part in your thoughts. You see, thoughts have their own energy signatures: The more powerful the continued thought, the more chance it has of turning into reality. No matter if they're positive or negative, all thoughts are accompanied by streams of prana, which in turn help transform those thoughts into reality. So be careful how and what you think!

The following exercises are meant to be used with the rhythmic breathing technique, in which you use the act of counting with inhaling, holding, and exhaling each breath. These are powerful exercises, yet they can be done easily and correctly. As before, if you experience dizziness or feel light-headed, please stop the exercise and take a break until your system gets used to breathing in this manner.

Take your time, and try to focus on doing the exercises properly so that you'll obtain astonishing benefits from them—but keep in mind that getting into the *rhythm* of the breath is more important than striving for the *duration* of the breath.

Exercise

Find a comfortable place to lie down flat, perhaps on a bed or a mat on the floor. Rest your hands lightly over your solar plexus and breathe rhythmically. Inhale slowly to the count of four; hold that for two counts, and exhale to the count of four. After another two counts, breathe in again for four counts, hold for two counts, and breathe out to the count of four. Continue for five minutes, until you've settled into a steady rhythm that will be used throughout this exercise.

After you've established a comfortable rhythm, I want you to use your imagination to picture each incoming breath infused with prana. Remember that you can command prana just like yogis do to flow wherever you wish. (Some people may also find it helpful to visualize prana in the form of sparkling-white light.)

With each breath, try to create a mental picture of the prana rushing in through your nostrils and flowing right down into your lungs. Imagine this energy flowing, being absorbed by and stored in your solar plexus. With each breath, let the energy circulate in your solar-plexus area, as it builds and strengthens your total body and mind.

As you exhale, visualize this precious energy being distributed all over your body. Feel it in every bone, muscle, and nerve ending, from the top of your head to the very tips of your fingers and toes. This exercise is wonderful if you're feeling tired, or if you want to revitalize yourself. You may experience a tingling sensation on your scalp, forehead, face, or even in your hands and fingers. This is quite normal, and it's a positive sign that you're feeling the effects of the prana, and that you're doing the exercise correctly. You may also feel the energy moving back and forth as it cleanses and revitalizes you; at the same time, it's raising your vibration and replenishing your vital supply of psychic energy. Once again, don't force this exercise: It should be carried out with a calm and gentle frame of mind in order to start you off as you work with your psychic breath.

Exercise

When you become proficient at recharging yourself, you'll be able to share this gift with family members or friends who are feeling lethargic or perhaps just under the weather.

Sit facing your friend and place your palms *over* his, making sure that your toes are also touching his. (You're forming a sort of conduit so that your energy can be circulated and shared.) Start to breathe in a rhythmic pattern and encourage the other person to follow your lead. Explain the count system carefully and slowly, keeping in mind that it's always good to start off with the four/two/four count in the beginning—that is, breathe in for four counts, hold for two counts, and breathe out for four counts. Do this for a while to get the rhythm going;

after about five minutes, you and your friend should be following the exact same breathing pattern.

Now I want you to visualize the prana flowing into your system and filling your entire being. Then send it to the other person—imagine that it's a sparkling golden light being taken in through his hands and feet, steadily spreading throughout his entire body. Have your friend imagine that he's receiving and taking in this vital energy as it circulates through his entire body.

Try this for ten minutes (at first). When the exercise is complete, remove your palms and breathe rhythmically, independent of each other for a few minutes. Take your time before you both get up, and end the session by washing your hands to break the connection with each other.

Manifesting Your Goals

How do we make our dreams come true? Once we have clear pictures in our minds (which, of course, should serve the highest good of all), we can give these desires an extra boost by sending a charged psychic breath to help them take flight. Our mind is far more than a mere storage library—it's a finely tuned creative instrument that can assist us in shaping our own reality and future. So please keep in mind that this exercise is meant to help you on a physical as well as a spiritual level.

Our confidence has a tendency to take a big leap forward each and every time we achieve a goal, so I find it helpful to start off with small things rather than to take on longer, complicated objectives. So begin by thinking about particular goals that you've been putting off, and write them down in your journal. Which ones would help you alleviate stress and make you feel better? Would taking a meditation class, cleaning your home, or devoting special time to yourself or your family help? By working on smaller, more obtainable aims in the beginning, you'll strengthen your ability to achieve the bigger dreams that you may have in the future.

The universe wants you to be healthy, happy, and to live in abundance; at the same time, you have to work at meeting your desires and goals halfway. I mean, you can't expect to sit back with no effort and say, "Okay, Universe, bring it on!" You have to charge your thoughts and actively keep them in mind by controlling your will while you work toward your desire. Then and only then can you expect changes in your life to develop. Also, your inner guidance may place you at the right place at the right time for an answer or new direction to present itself, so it's time for the next exercise, some of which should now be familiar to you.

Exercise

Sit or lie down comfortably, and start with the rhythmic breathing technique. Count in a way that is now comfortable for you (as before, I recommend the four/two/four count), bringing the prana into your solar plexus for five to ten minutes.

Now picture the steps that are required to achieve your goal. Most important, I want you to see the final resolution of your goal, and then feel what it's like to have a successful outcome already, as if it's happening right now. Feel the excitement, energy, and happiness as you imagine yourself in this perfect scenario.

As you focus on and hold this image, send the stored prana from your solar plexus to the desired outcome in order to increase its energy. Stay with this image until you feel that it's been fully charged. When you feel that you're ready, let the image go and release it to the universe. In the following days or weeks, try to notice if anything shifted positively with respect to your goal becoming a reality. In other words, are new steps or people beginning to appear in your life who are helping you get closer to attaining your goal? Write down your experience in your journal, and remember that anything is possible when you have faith, trust, and the power of the universe to back it up!

The power and uses of psychic breathing are boundless. Once again, please remember that this technique can assist you in bringing vital energy to any part of your body that needs healing and attention. You can support any healing process by directing pranic energy to a specific area. As time goes on and you become more proficient with psychic breathing, you can increase the duration of the counts. Enjoy experimenting and working with your breath, for it can be an enlightening and uplifting way to get to know yourself and *all* that you can be. This is your time to unlock your full potential.

Affirmations:

"Breath is power."

"Psychic energy is real and attainable."

The Human Psychic Atmosphere

Have you ever met someone for the first time, when from out of nowhere, images and feelings just poured into your mind? It's times like these when you absolutely know whether or not you're going to like that person. It's often a very strong feeling—you may form a picture of them, have a sense of what they do for a living, or you may pick up certain people and conditions that are around the person. In the split second during that first introduction, you get a total "download" of all sorts of information, as your mind begins to try to decipher what you're receiving. What's really going on is that you're actually reading and interpreting the person's *aura*.

What Is an Aura?

You've probably seen religious paintings of saints and angels with golden halos around their heads, which represent the spiritual light of the aura. However, you don't have to be a saint or an angel—we all have our own unique aura.

Over the years, auras have been described in a variety of ways. To put it as simply as I can, they're the energy fields that surround all matter. The human aura, which surrounds the physical body, emanates in all directions, is usually oval in shape, and manifests itself as a magnetic field. This energy constantly flows and changes according to our moods and emotional, mental, and physical states. Even our personal history gets imprinted on our aura, including our memories, ideas, goals, physical ailments, and who we really are. No medical record could ever contain so much information.

Auras are comprised of various *auric layers,* and the more psychically sensitive we are, the more likely we'll be able to see and feel more of these layers. Yet few of us ever realize that we're sensing auras of both people and places, even though we all have the capacity to do so. For example:

- Have you ever been in line at the post office and sensed when someone stepped behind you?
- Have you felt someone staring at you from across a room?
- Do you notice when you feel comfortable or uncomfortable in certain rooms?
- Do certain colors affect you in different ways?
- Do you feel energized by some people, while others leave you feeling drained?

All of the above are signs of experiencing an aura. I believe that our primitive ancestors relied on these energy fields to sense when danger was present. After all, they had no other detection system, so they had to depend on their own senses and their own abilities to judge whether someone or something was friend or foe. Over time, we've gradually lost some of this raw sensory ability, but it's possible to learn how to use it again. Many young children see auras, which explains why they often draw people in various hues of color. They may draw their mom in yellow or their dad in green or their best friend in layers of brightly different colors—they're observing the world as it *really* is.

The intensity of the color and the brightness of the aura itself will reflect the state of a person's health, vitality, and mental and emotional condition. Every aura is uniquely different and vibrates to its own individual frequency. It's possible that with practice, you'll be able to increase your auric vibration and also learn how to expand it or draw it in closer to you. When your aura is open and you're vibrating at the same frequency with someone else or a physical place, that's when you'll sense a connection; when you don't resonate with someone, it's because you're both vibrating at a different levels. This is why you may feel a sense of disconnection, or what I like to refer to as *bumping auras*. Other times it may take you a little while to blend with someone else's energy before both of you feel comfortable with each other.

During my training, I quickly learned that if you're going to work with your energy field, then you need to understand it. I remember those two intense years in England when I needed to meet people who could help me in my quest to further my education and knowledge of mediumship. Since I'd never been to the UK, I didn't know which direction to take in my search for like-minded people or teachers. However, all my thoughts were focused on seeking out these people, and as *all* thoughts are contained within the aura, it wasn't long before I began to attract individuals who pointed me in the right direction. Many of these people weren't necessarily into metaphysics, but it was often the case that they somehow knew someone or had read an article that helped me achieve my goal.

You've heard the saying "Like attracts like"—well, it's really more about *frequency attracting the same frequency*. As I've said, everything is made up of energy, and that includes you and me. Since we're energy, it's probable that we'll tune in to and attract the same frequency that we're resonating. That's why you should be careful of your thoughts (positive or negative)—your aura is magnetic, so if you continually think about something, it's almost guaranteed that you'll ultimately attract it.

Psychic awareness can be enhanced once you become aware of the aura and its many uses. I recommend that you learn all you can about auras to help you physically and spiritually.

Here are a few benefits of working with auras, and how they can work *with* you and *for* you:

- They will expand your intuitive psychic abilities.

- You will maintain a healthier body.

- You will be able to find like-minded people and spiritually beneficial places quickly.

- You will be able to protect your personal space.

- You will begin to attract positive people and conditions that can assist you in all areas of your life.

As I explained in Chapter 2, some people may use their clairvoyance to see an aura, whereas clairaudients will hear certain words about it, and clairsentients will feel or sense it. No matter what psychic sense you feel is the strongest, you can absolutely discover the best way to understand and read an aura.

Affirmations:

"Auras are real, and I can sense them."

"I am now attracting all that I need in my life for my highest good."

Developing Auric Vision

I believe that some people are *attracted* to light, while others *emanate* it. I once had an incredible experience that validates this phenomenon when I was demonstrating my mediumship to an eagerly awaiting audience at the Omega Institute in Rhinebeck, New York. As usual, I started my demonstration by explaining to the audience how I work as a spirit messenger and link with those who have passed over. I always discuss the quickening process, in which I raise my vibrations and Spirit lowers theirs, enabling us to blend together. However, even before I had a chance to finish explaining the delicate process on this particular evening, I was totally drawn to a woman in the middle of the audience. I couldn't take my eyes off her.

Now it's important to stress here that when I demonstrate my mediumship and deliver messages from loved ones on the Other Side, I really have no idea whom I'll be drawn to, what the connection with the audience member will be, or the nature of the message. Yet this woman seemed to be glowing, as if from the inside out. It was an extraordinary sight, and I was conscious that I was witnessing something quite unique. The rest of the audience seemed to fade around her, as I observed a luminous, dazzling light emanating from all around her. Her aura was literally beaming! To this day, I've never seen anyone else so beautifully illuminated.

It turns out that her name was Elizabeth, and I quickly established that her husband had passed away some years before. He was a gentle spirit, and his love was evident in his beautiful message for her that night, which flowed easily and effortlessly as she sat there, smiling and nodding her head. It turns out that Elizabeth had enrolled in the workshop hoping to hear from her husband, and she certainly got her wish. I knew that he was standing right beside her and that his energy and love had somehow amplified her auric light. Later that evening, other people who had been sitting near Elizabeth expressed how they'd felt a tingling sensation, for they too were blending with her aura and feeling the emanations of this lovely woman and her husband.

One of the most popular segments I teach in my workshops is how to see auras. Now, I don't want to mislead you into thinking that you're going to wake up one day and start seeing these energy fields; nor is it possible to just read a book and suddenly be able to see them. However, once you realize that you're not necessarily viewing auras with your *physical* eyes, but with your *psychic inner* eye, then you'll have a better understanding of how to see the auric light that surrounds everyone and everything. I find it helpful to imagine yourself as a being of light and energy, because in reality, you are!

Exercise

To increase your chances of viewing an aura, I suggest that you find a dim room with as little direct sunlight as possible. (You may be able to use your special place if the lighting is adjustable.) You'll also need a blank wall for a friend to stand in front of, which should preferably be a neutral color such as tan or white and free from pictures or ornaments. When viewing someone's aura, it's best to have them wear pale, light colors.

Begin by closing your eyes and taking a few deep breaths. Once you're relaxed, bring your awareness up to your third eye.

(I believe that the aura is a type of "viewing screen" for your third eye, and with practice, you'll be able to strengthen your vision to see auras all the time.) As you open your physical eyes, keep your awareness on the point between your brows, which doesn't mean that you should roll your eyes up into your head. Take your time here.

Have your friend sit or stand in front of the blank wall. Position yourself far enough away so that you can see her entire body. Remember that you're looking at her with your psychic eye, so keep your awareness between your brows. Start by looking at the space just to the side of your friend's head and shoulders; that is, look past her. She should only be in your peripheral vision—don't struggle to focus on her.

Allow your eyes to relax as you continue to look at the space *beside* your friend. Now, by using your breath, continue to hold your awareness in your third-eye area and ask your friend to slowly rock back and forth. You should begin to notice a whitish-blue glow form around her head-and-shoulder area, which should mirror her rocking movement. Try to observe if the aura is larger in one area than another or if there are any hints of color around it. Many psychic impressions can be seen and felt in the aura, so at this point, let any intuitive information flow. When you're finished, write down these experiences in your journal. If you feel comfortable talking at the same time, try telling your friend what you're seeing so that she can give you her feedback.

To finish this exercise, close your eyes, take a breath, and bring your awareness back down to your physical eyes. Take a moment to relax and breathe; now try switching places to let your partner see *your* aura.

As I said, you're not going to wake up one day and immediately be able to see auras. If you don't see anything right away, that's okay—you're learning a new way to see, so take your time and don't give up. (When I first started, it took me some time to get it right.) Keep practicing this exercise. Once you see your first aura, you'll suddenly start noticing them all the time with less effort. In time, you'll be able to expand your auric vision to see more profound levels, and the colors will intensify and become more visible.

And don't limit your practice to people—try to see the auras of plants and trees outside as well. I remember one particularly clear, deep blue, and cloudless day, when I saw the aura of a pine tree for the first time. I stood there for several minutes, transfixed. It created a visual memory that I've never forgotten.

Affirmations:

"I am now awakening my natural ability to see auras."

"I am beginning to be aware of the vibrations that surround everyone and everything."

Aura Colors and Their Meanings

It's often said that we're a rainbow of colors: Every color has its own meaning, and each can affect us in uniquely different and profound ways. This is most applicable when it comes to the topic of the colors in our aura. The hues in our individual energy field constantly change as we go through life, reflecting our health, emotions, mood, frame of mind, and level of spiritual well-being.

Typically, there's more than one color in an individual's aura—as you develop your skills, you should start to notice this. Bright colors usually signify a healthier and positive disposition, while dull shades can reflect the opposite. There are no set standards for interpreting the colors of an aura, as they mean different things to different people.

I've developed my own standard interpretations over years of practice. For example, when I see green in someone's aura, it usually signifies that they're under medical care, are going through a process of healing, or are healers themselves; yet green to someone else may mean that the subject has a very calming personality. When interpreting the aura, you must combine your intuition and psychic ability to understand what you're seeing and feeling. Over time, as you increase your abilities even further, you'll know what colors particular people need to incorporate or boost in their aura—

as well as your own. You may want to ask, "Is there a certain color I need in my life?" You might also begin noticing what colors you're attracted to, which ones you have in your home, and also which ones you're wearing right now.

Following is a quick summary of just some of the meanings of each color. This is by no means a comprehensive explanation, but it's a useful starting point. You may want to add the meaning of colors in your journal and write down your favorite one—but more important, note how each one makes you feel. Once you begin to understand and work with colors, understanding how they affect and influence your life, you'll never look at them in the same way again.

Red

The color red symbolizes vitality, passion, temper, strength, survival, hard work, and leadership. It's a very physical color, and many athletes and successful businesspeople are likely to reflect some in their aura. When you feel tired, try bringing a little red into your aura to give you that useful boost in energy. However, too much red can make you hyperactive or oversensitive.

Orange

Creativity and joyous emotions are embodied in this color. People who have orange in their aura are often very independent, personable, and open-minded, and they're easy to communicate with. Orange is about spreading happiness, joy, and emotional pleasures, as well as the vitality that's associated with these things.

Yellow

The color yellow represents wisdom, mental force, curiosity, insight, intuition, and sensitivity. People who have yellow in their auras are most likely the ones who can light up a room with their positive energy. When someone begins to develop both psychically and spiritually, particularly with their clairsentient ability, yellow will often be one of the strongest colors in their aura. It's a sign of a positive attitude.

Green

Love, health, balance, compassion, a nurturing nature, and abundance are many of the qualities of green. It both calms and refreshes your energy, and is a sign of renewal and growth. The color green is also a strong reflection of someone who's practicing some form of healing, whether on others or themselves.

Blue

Blue symbolizes communication, speech, expression, imagination, and freedom. When I notice this color in someone's aura, they usually have a positive spiritual outlook on life. Also, those who are highly developed psychically will reflect this color, as blue signifies the ability of clairaudience. Blue will calm and bring peace to those who focus on incorporating this color into their aura.

Indigo

Inner wisdom and perception, as well as a vivid imagination, are reflected in the color of indigo. When this color is dominant in someone's aura, he or she is more than likely already practicing some form of spirituality and can look at problems and issues from a higher, intuitive view. Indigo signifies the ability of clairvoyance.

Violet

One of the most spiritual colors, violet reflects higher wisdom, beauty, inspiration, creativity, and enlightenment. People with violet in their auras are usually not very materialistic and are focused on their spiritual development. I suggest that such individuals follow a creative career and open themselves and their spirit to the color violet for inspiration and guidance.

White

Symbolizing truth, innocence, and purity, white is one of the colors that you're most likely to see when you start developing your auric vision. It could appear almost transparent, but white reflects *all* the colors within it and is the color of the universal energy (prana). Sometimes when I'm working as a psychic medium, I see white specks of light around my sitters' heads, and there have been times when the link is so strong that they see the specks around me.

Brown

People who have brown in their aura are usually generous, down-to-earth, calm, organized, and inquisitive—they like to explore new concepts and ideas. Environmental issues and being outdoors in nature seem to be the top priority when this color is present. Using the color brown can keep you grounded and in the present, as well as helping you focus on the needs of today, rather than focusing on what might be tomorrow.

Black

People get nervous if you see black in their aura, even though it's made up from the entire color spectrum and can be a protective color. Here's where you'll need to use your intuitive ability to access what black means to you, but don't let your imagination run away with you. If this color is predominant, then it could (and I stress *could*) mean an illness or fatigue. For example, I was reading for someone, and I saw black dots above his head. I later found out that he was dealing with severe depression and was taking medication for it. If this applies to you or someone you know and there is due concern, then seek professional advice from a therapist or doctor before second-guessing.

Gold

I've always felt that gold is the most powerful color, as it's a sign of protection. If you're nervous entering a particular place or are approaching a challenging situation, try surrounding yourself with bright gold. People who are blessed with an abundance of gold in their auras radiate spirituality and inspire others to work as spiritual teachers or leaders themselves.

Affirmations:

"The world of color is opening to me every day."

*"I safely choose all the colors I
need to enhance my life and spirit."*

Sensing the Aura

Auras really do exist—even if you can't see them. It may be that you're more clairsentient and have a stronger ability to feel rather than see an aura. You may have noticed that when healers work on someone's aura, they tend to move their hands over the body, smoothing and healing its energy field. The hands are wonderful receptors of energy, and it's possible to obtain psychic insight and impressions in this way when sensing and working with the aura. As I've explained in this chapter, the aura extends far beyond your physical body—so now you'll start to notice those times when you approach a place or a situation that doesn't feel right to you. You'll become more aware when you're at a gathering and find yourself drawn to a certain person, or when you feel you need to distance yourself from someone. When you find yourself in these situations, stop and notice how you're feeling, what you're sensing, and even what colors you perceive. By doing so, you'll give your inner guidance a chance to give you some psychic insight that may be quite useful in that situation.

You can learn to *expand* your aura. There are many reasons why you'd want to do this: Perhaps you're about to do a psychic reading, go to a concert and want to feel more of the music, or are outdoors and just want to heighten the whole experience with nature. To repeat one more time, we're all made up of energy, so you can blend your aura with another person, a place, a plant, or even your trusted pet.

You can also *contract* (pull back) your aura if you want to be less sensitive. I remember when I used to travel to work on the crowded subway that it was easy to absorb all the energy from everyone around me, so it was important to contract my aura. I'd simply imagine that my aura was tight around me before entering the train, and I'd arrive at work feeling calm and refreshed.

You can pull back, recharge, and expand your aura in any number of ways, from the use of breath, meditation, bringing color into your aura, or thought. The advantages of understanding and knowing you're in control of your aura are limitless.

In the next two exercises, we'll learn how to feel the auric energy surrounding the human body.

Exercise

As always, get comfortable first. Take a seat or stand in a comfortable position. Take in a deep cleansing breath, let it out, and relax. Now breathe in and let it out once again.

Rub the palms of your hands together briskly for about 20 to 30 seconds. This will make your hands even more sensitive and receptive. Place your palms about a foot in front of you so that they're facing each other. Slowly bring your palms together, pull them apart again, and bring them back together. Don't let the palms touch, and keep the distance at about 12 inches each time as you pull them apart.

You should begin to notice a slight pressure developing, like two magnets repelling each other. You may also feel a slight temperature change or a tingling sensation. You can even create a ball of energy between your hands. Other people may also feel this energy if they were to slowly run the palm of their hand between yours.

This is a great exercise to assist you in feeling your energy field, as well as others'; with continued practice, your hands will become highly tuned receptors for those subtle vibrations that emanate from everything, including yourself. (And as always, write down your experience in your psychic journal.)

Let's take it one step further. I'm going to show you how to sense someone's aura and pick up some psychic sensations and impressions. In my workshop, this exercise requires two people working together, so you'll need your trusted friend again, and a low-back chair.

Exercise

Decide between the two of you who will be the "sitter" and who will be the "feeler" (for the purposes of this example, let's have you be the feeler). The sitter should take a seat with her feet flat on the floor, palms facing upward on her lap. Both of you should then take a breath and relax. You should be standing just behind the chair, with a straight, relaxed posture. Take a nice, slow breath, and rub your palms together (as we did in the previous exercise) for about 15 seconds.

Now the sitter should start thinking about something unpleasant that happened to her in the past, while you place your palms, starting at the top of her head, about ten inches away. *Slowly* move your hands around the sitter's head without touching it. Then move down to her shoulder area, pushing in your palms and slowly pulling them out and back in again. (It's important to concentrate so that you notice where the aura starts and how far it extends.) You should start to be aware of the sensation in your hands at this point. See if you can feel whether the sitter's aura has expanded—or is it still tight around her? Can you notice any temperature changes? If so, where are you noticing them? Are there any colors you can sense or feel? Keep a mental note so that you can explain it all to the sitter afterward.

Now I want you to hold your hands in one position (preferably a few inches above the sitter's head). Close your eyes and focus on your third-eye area to see if you can pick up what the sitter is thinking about. What has caused this unpleasant situation? Are you receiving any images or colors? You may even see a situation in your own life that will reflect her thought. The sitter can now surround that thought with white light and release it (after all, it's just a memory from the past); at the same time, you should shake off your hands toward the floor, away from you and the sitter. The energy will be absorbed and cleansed by the earth. *Do not* relay the information that you received just yet.

Now I want the sitter to think of one of the happiest days of her life. Go through the exercise again, just as above. You should rub your palms together and begin to feel the aura around her head and shoulders. Are there any changes? Did her aura contract or expand? Is the temperature different? Have the colors changed? Are your hands feeling more sensitive with that tingling sensation? With your hands in one position again, see if you can feel any impression as to what the sitter's happiest day was. Shake off the energy from your hands, and share all the information you gathered with the sitter. (Keep in mind that feedback is essential when developing your psychic sensitivity to see if you're on track.)

Switch places so that the sitter has a chance to feel and understand your aura. At the end of this exercise, both of you should wash your hands to totally break the connection. Please remember that everyone's aura is different—but this is a great way of increasing your psychic sensitivity as well as your confidence in feeling and interpreting auras without even seeing one.

Affirmations:

"I am a highly tuned piece of psychic equipment."
"I am now aware of all my psychic potential."

Strengthening the Aura

Many of us are drawn to the sea and are constantly seeking out the nearest coastline. Have you ever been to the beach and noticed how acutely aware you feel afterward—

along with the fact that you're simultaneously relaxed and invigorated? It's not just the sun or the sound of those crashing waves that are responsible. Both the salt from the ocean and the air combine to *ionize* your aura, cleansing and strengthening it, and leaving you feeling refreshed. It's almost as if all your problems have been washed away. No wonder bath salts are such a hit!

A strong, well-balanced, and cleansed aura is essential to everyone, both on a physical and spiritual level—that's why I've dedicated an entire chapter to the importance of learning and understanding all about this special energy source. We should consciously strive to achieve a powerful auric field, since we're constantly bombarded by external influences. Your aura can be affected by your state of mind and body, your emotions, the people around you, and your immediate environment; and if it becomes weak, you'll probably feel tired or drained, or in the most severe cases, you may feel powerless to make choices or decisions. If this continues, physical symptoms will become noticeable, as will mental and emotional imbalances. In these cases, as always, seek out the advice of your doctor.

Your aura is a wonderful early-detection system. It will alert you early on, so you'll have time to do something about it. And when it's healthy and strong, it acts as a protective shield. Your aura can be strengthened in a number of different ways. It doesn't require a lot of work and can help you stay healthy, improve your psychic abilities, keep you safe, and attract only what's best for you.

I'm sure it goes without saying that regular physical exercise and being outdoors in the sunshine, breathing in fresh air rich in oxygen and prana, will help strengthen and revitalize your aura. So if you work in an air-conditioned office with artificial lights, really make an effort to go out for a short walk at lunchtime, even if it's just for ten minutes. I strongly advocate that everyone should complement what nature provides with various types of healing. Massage, Reiki, therapeutic touch, polarity, aromatherapy, and acupuncture will all greatly reinforce and replenish your energy field—but be sure that you find what works and feels the best *for you*.

Diet and a healthy lifestyle play a big part in keeping your aura balanced, and as I constantly preach, you should do everything in moderation. Too much alcohol, tobacco, or the dreaded fast food will have a negative effect on your aura and will weaken your energy system.

Yet just being aware of your aura is a great start. You get dressed every morning to protect yourself from the elements, right? Well, this is a perfect time to just place a protective thought on your aura. Before you start your busy day, see your aura as a brilliant white light that acts as an invisible shield that surrounds and stays with you throughout your day and evening. Take time to rest and relax as much as possible—and of course, every time you meditate, you'll be building your psychic strength and reinforcing your precious aura.

Exercise

Earlier I talked about using the color gold for protection. Here's a short exercise to add additional protection to your aura so that only the best and highest good will be able to penetrate it. Try it for about ten minutes, or use it as a cleansing and strengthening technique. (This meditation can also be enhanced by using the psychic breathing technique from Chapter 4.)

Lie or sit in a comfortable position. Now close your eyes and imagine a bright, golden light just in front of you. See it slowly begin to grow and become larger and brighter. Imagine that you're breathing in this beautiful golden light, which is slowly entering your heart area. Keep your awareness there for a minute or two. Next I want you to focus your attention on the crown of your head—as you move your awareness here, bring the golden light with you. See it pouring out of you like a fountain that's totally surrounding you. Every time you breathe in this beautiful golden light, it will surround your whole aura to protect and strengthen it. I want you to imagine it as a luminous, oval-shaped circle. Use your breath to continue to bring in this golden light, which reinforces and strengthens your aura.

Repeat these words: "As I strengthen my aura, only positive energy can enter my space, and only positive energy can go out." Keep the golden light with you, and know that it's there anytime you need it to keep you strong, happy, whole, and safe.

Affirmations:

"Positive energy surrounds me at all times."
"I am now aware of the importance of protecting my aura."

CHAPTER

Spiritual Batteries

We humans are continually seeking out different places to find enlightenment, whether it's a church, a synagogue, or one of the many sacred locations all over the world. As we persistently search for our own spirit, we have a tendency to look outside ourselves. (I certainly don't undervalue the importance many people put on places of worship, as I often visit churches myself for the wisdom, peace, and solitude contained therein, which comforts and uplifts me.) But when we begin to understand and work with our chakra system, we'll soon realize and appreciate that our bodies are truly our temples.

I remember the first time I heard the word *chakra:* I was intrigued by every aspect of it, from the sound itself to its origins and meaning. Then and there I made a promise to myself that I'd discover and learn exactly what this fascinating word truly meant. Of course I didn't realize at the time what an important function chakras have to the overall well-being of each and every one of us. . . .

What Are Chakras?

The word *chakra* is a Sanskrit word meaning "wheel." Chakras are the energy centers of the body, but I often refer to them as our "spiritual batteries." Some people imagine them as beautiful lotuses with unfolding petals, while others who have developed their psychic sight may see chakras as vortexes of swirling light.

Evidence of these energy centers has been documented for thousands of years in the East. More recently here in the West, we've begun to investigate and research this precious energy system of the body. Over the years, everyone I've ever met or studied with—be they Eastern or Western—has all come to the same conclusion (which I also firmly believe): Human anatomy is engineered by a complex network of etheric wiring through which energy flows, and the chakras are the organizing centers for both the reception and the transmission of life energies (chi/prana), which are essential to our physical, mental, and spiritual development.

⊠ ⊠ ⊠

There are seven major chakras within and around you, each of which corresponds to an endocrine gland in your body. (You also have many minor chakras; however, during the early stages of your development, I suggest that you just focus on the main seven.) Chakras run upward along the spinal cord, and energy enters from both the front and back of each one. These seven centers are the link between your physical body and your aura, and they constantly interact with each other. Each chakra is also complemented by its own auric color and has its own unique function.

Chakras act as sensitive contact points, or a bridge, on which the physical and spiritual worlds meet. The lower chakras deal with the physical body and relate to issues of living in this physical world, such as survival, health, careers, safety, and the home; while the upper or higher chakras deal with all psychic abilities and spiritual gifts.

Now your actions and thoughts also play a big part in controlling your chakras' flow of energy, as well as their functions—so even though the energy that runs through these centers remains constant, it can be increased or decreased depending on how well you balance your life. For instance, if you're worrying about financial issues (which are purely "physical" concerns), then your lower chakras are likely to be affected in a negative way by slowing down their rate and spin. When this happens, the disbursement of energy will be weaker; as a result, you may feel sluggish or out of balance.

However, if you're feeling compassionate toward someone or are focusing on higher spiritual thoughts, then your upper chakras are more likely to spin freely, resulting in the energy being dispersed freely and with it a sense of balance and vitality. In other words, there has to be *balance* when you activate and work with your chakras—you should never focus on stimulating just one. All seven chakras should be in balance so that the flow of energy can travel through them evenly to the appropriate areas.

I believe that we're meant to have unlimited amounts of energy; we should also be able to tap in to our creative talents easily and live a life of love, compassion, and peace. It's possible to have all this once we turn inward, allowing the natural balance of energy to flow through our spiritual batteries, where transformation truly begins.

In the following sections, you'll learn more about the chakras and how essential they are to your health, spirituality, inner guidance system . . . and your life.

Affirmations:

"My body is my temple."
"I am now becoming aware of each chakra."

The Seven Energy Centers

Every chakra has a set of related colors, sounds, and glands, as well as key words that will make it resonate. Understanding and learning these reference points will greatly enhance and support a greater physical and spiritual understanding.

Let's now look at all seven chakras.

1. The Base or Root Chakra

- *Color:* Red
- *Sound:* Lam
- *Gland:* Adrenals
- *Key words:* "I have"

Situated at the base of the spine, the base or root chakra is most closely related to all earthly issues such as survival, the physical body, and financial concerns, as well as sustenance, safety, and shelter.

When the energy of this chakra is blocked or depleted, you may have a sense of not feeling totally grounded. This could cause you to say, "I don't feel quite right today" or "Lately, I'm just not feeling like myself."

You may also experience fatigue, feel lethargic or unmotivated, be prone to seek approval, or be overly cautious. An overactive first chakra, on the other hand, may cause you to suffer from anger or feel unduly physically aggressive, impulsive, hyperactive, or even reckless.

To balance this chakra, yoga is highly beneficial, and dancing or light physical exercise like tai chi will assist in keeping the energy flowing and balanced. If you're feeling slightly spacey, try imagining roots spreading from the base of your spine and digging themselves into the earth like a tree. I know this sounds a little crazy, but this simple thought has the power to keep you grounded in the present.

Finally, keep in mind that honoring your body and taking care of it on the *outside* will benefit you *inside*. It works both ways!

2. The Sacral Chakra

- *Color:* Orange
- *Sound:* Vam
- *Gland:* Testicles, ovaries
- *Key words:* "I want"

Located two fingers below the navel, the sacral chakra relates to emotions, desires, creativity, and sexuality. An underactive sacral chakra can cause you to experience a lower sexual drive, or you may become introverted and worry about what others think of you. Yet if it's overactive, then you'll feel sexually aggressive, jealous, or possessive, or you may suffer from lower back pain or kidney problems.

When your sacral chakra is balanced, you'll enjoy life and all it has to offer with passion and excitement. So, to keep the energy flowing, try different forms of dance in which you move your hips and your lower abdomen. Use a color meditation, practice yoga, express your sexuality, and nurture yourself. Remember, you *do* matter!

3. The Solar-Plexus Chakra

- *Color:* Yellow
- *Sound:* Ram
- *Gland:* Pancreas, adrenals
- *Key words:* "I can"

Located between the navel area and the rib cage, the solar-plexus chakra represents power, vitality, self-control, self-esteem, and confidence. This is the center where all your emotions and feelings are recorded; it's also associated with clairsentience, as it's a major psychic reception area. When developing psychically, you should be aware of this sensitive area and learn how to "close down" properly so that you avoid becoming too sensitive or receiving unwanted energies from people or certain places. (See the exercise on page 129 for details on how to do this.)

When this chakra is balanced, you'll appear really confident, as though you're ready to take on the world; when it's unbalanced, you'll become judgmental, have a tendency to plan things without following through, worry too much, and suffer from nervous exhaustion. Stomach problems and digestive disorders, including ulcers, are common to this area when it's unbalanced.

To balance this chakra, you may want to try energy healing with a professional—workshops and classes that focus on self-empowerment can greatly help open and balance this area. It's also helpful to do breath work complemented with color. (And be aware of people who *take* your energy.)

4. The Heart Chakra

- *Color:* Green
- *Sound:* Yam
- *Gland:* Thymus
- *Key words:* "I love"

Found right where its name indicates, the heart chakra represents unconditional love, compassion, joy, balance, relationships, and healing. It's said to be the link between our mind/body and spirit.

This chakra is associated with the human heart, so it's often filled with so much joy and happiness. Emotions flow so strongly through here that it's possible you'll find tears rolling down your face when you meditate. This is also the area where all past hurts, disappointments, and emotional scars reside, so as energy reaches this area, it will try to move and help clear any blockages you may have.

By balancing this area, emotions that relate to past issues can be healed, which will then enable you to move on with your life; however, if left unbalanced, anger, jealousy, and heart conditions can develop. An underactive heart chakra will cause you to experience self-worth issues, feelings of being unloved, or a lack of compassion.

Balancing this area may take a while—be sure to take all the time you need so that the healing energy can get through and flow freely to your other chakras. Loving yourself and others, performing acts of compassion, and learning forgiveness, as well as being outdoors and surrounding yourself with the beauty of nature, will help balance this area. A breath facilitator (a professional trained and certified in the art of *conscious breathing*) and a therapist or counselor can assist you in working through blockages in your heart chakra for overall well-being and emotional healing.

5. The Throat Chakra

- *Color:* Light blue
- *Sound:* Ham
- *Gland:* Thyroid
- *Key words:* "I speak"

Located, as you might expect, in the throat area, the throat chakra is associated with communication, sound, creativity, and the ability of clairaudience. Many artists, speakers, writers, singers, and other creative individuals often have active throat chakras.

Have you ever noticed someone who's constantly clearing their throat? When I observe this, I usually ask the person if they need to say something. You see, people have a way of holding back what needs to be said; in doing so, they can cause an "energy backup" in the throat area—hence the saying, "They were choking on their words." When the throat chakra is unbalanced, sore throats, skin irritations, and ear infections are common, and tension creeps into the neck and shoulder areas. When it's underactive, you're likely to resist change, appear slow to respond, or easily surrender yourself to others.

By activating and balancing this center, it will inspire you to speak and listen to the truth, both for yourself as well as others. To do so, try humming, chanting, or singing out loud; and most important, if you have something to say, please *speak up!* (And don't be surprised if you suddenly become creatively inspired.)

6. The Third-Eye Chakra

- *Color:* Indigo
- *Sound:* Om
- *Gland:* Pituitary
- *Key words:* "I see"

The third-eye chakra, which is the one that's most talked about, is associated with clairvoyance, intuition, and higher levels of consciousness. Found between the brows and just above the bridge of your nose, this chakra works closely with the throat and crown chakras to assist you with your psychic and intuitive inner guidance. Most psychics, artists, and people with vivid imaginations often have a well-developed third eye; with the proper development, you too will be able to "see" far beyond ordinary sight to find solutions and choices that aren't necessarily right in front of you. Otherwise, if this chakra stays underdeveloped, you may be afraid of success and unable to see the bigger picture, which is often a result of not being able to visualize yourself as happy and successful.

When this center is unbalanced, you could experience eyestrain, vision problems, worrying, headaches, or forgetfulness. I know that when I'm doing too much psychic work, I experience a band of tightness around my head, which is a sign that my third-eye chakra is overactive and I need to go to the gym—it's time to bring the energy back down into my lower chakras for balance.

To balance the third-eye chakra, I recommend walking meditations, breath work, visualizations, and color. Don't just focus on this one chakra as part of your development; instead, it's important to remember that *all* of them must be in balance so that they can work in unison and harmony.

7. The Crown Chakra

- *Color:* Violet
- *Sound:* Silence
- *Gland:* Pineal
- *Key words:* "I know"

Located at the top of the head and also known as "The Thousand-Petaled Lotus" or "The Receiver of Light," the crown chakra is the center of your link with the Universe and your higher consciousness; in other words, it's the connection with wisdom and spiritual insight. The crown center is where spiritual light and energy are received and then dispersed throughout your aura for your total well-being.

When this chakra is stimulated and balanced, energy can flow up the spine and out through this center, like a beautiful fountain that washes over you with positive energy, lifting up your spirit. When left unbalanced, feelings of being cut off, frustrated, depressed, unhappy, or full of doubt can develop. You may even experience writer's block—in this case, energy doesn't flow freely into the center, resulting in a lack of inspiration. However, when properly balanced, the crown chakra will expand to a point where it's possible to access and tap in to the deepest sources of universal wisdom.

To balance this chakra, try meditation, breath work, yoga, spiritual healing, acupuncture, and color.

Affirmations for All the Chakras:

"I am energy."

"The Universe flows through me and guides me."

Chakra Workouts

Sound, color, vibration, breath, and thought each play an important role in balancing and stimulating the chakras. In this section, I'll explain the different ways in which you can keep your energy flowing freely to each and every one of your chakras so that they can work together.

Since chakras are the gateways to your psychic and intuitive abilities, by keeping them cleansed and well-balanced you'll also heighten your psychic awareness. This will then make it easier for you to discern the impressions that are being sent from your inner guidance to your physical consciousness.

As I've already explained, each of the seven chakras relates to a certain part of your body, so any imbalances or blockages may affect the corresponding area, resulting in physical ailments or disease. For example, my friend Peter ran his own company for many years, but there was a time when the economy took a serious dip. Concerned that there wouldn't be enough money in the bank to keep the company afloat or to pay his staff, Peter started to suffer from major back pain.

Monetary issues can physically manifest in the base chakra (survival). Peter's financial worry had caused his base chakra to get thrown out of balance, and the blockage and imbalance surfaced as back pain. Have you ever heard the expression, "I feel like I'm carrying the weight of the world"? Well, in a sense, Peter was. Through massage, acupuncture, and of course, good financial advice, he was able to release the blocked energy and start the gradual healing process that he so greatly needed. As a postscript, his business not only survived, it flourished!

⊠ ⊠ ⊠

The chakras relate to how you interact and live in the world. They can be opened and closed, balanced, stimulated, and healed depending on the need. The following techniques will help you embark on your journey of discovering and nurturing your precious energy system and spiritual batteries.

Exercise

I learned the following technique from a medium while I was studying in the UK—it's very simple, and can be done every day if you wish.

The next time you take a shower, imagine that the refreshing water is infused with a healing white light. As you stand under the water, keep your left hand on the bottom of your lower back, then place the right hand in front of you over your sacral chakra (just below the navel). Start circulating your right hand in a counterclockwise motion, imagining that you're moving the energy and cleansing this entire center. Keep your left hand on the base chakra throughout.

Now move your right hand up to your solar-plexus chakra, and once again begin to move the energy in a circular, counterclockwise movement. Continue to do so with the remaining chakras, until you reach your crown chakra on top of your head. This simple technique helps you cleanse and balance your chakras, as the cleansing and invigorating wash will make you more aware of your energy centers just by placing a thought and intention on each one. Give it a try!

Colors have their own unique energy patterns as well as their own frequencies, so the chakras will resonate and radiate the energy of their individual hue as well. In the previous section, I listed the chakra colors, which are red, orange, yellow, green, blue, indigo, and violet. I know it's easy to forget the colors or which order they're in, so here's an easy tip that I use: Remember the following gentleman's name, "Roy G. Biv." If you notice, each letter in the name begins with the order of the color sequence for the chakras. (You can also easily make up your own memory jogger.)

Using colors with the breath will balance, heal, and enhance your chakras' individual functions and will assist the psychic energy in flowing to your whole being. Now try the following technique.

Exercise

Sit or lie comfortably, close your eyes, and relax. (I recommend using the Complete Breath technique I described in Chapter 4.) Imagine that a small, shimmering red cloud is right in front of you. As you take in a breath, it now enters through your nostrils and slowly fills your lungs with its beautiful color. As you exhale, you may want to imagine it leaving through the base chakra on the out breath. Continue to breathe, moving the color to the base of your spine. Take your time, staying with the chakra for as long as you feel you need to.

Now, one by one, move on to the rest of the chakras, using their corresponding colors. Notice how the cloud of color changes with each chakra. For example, at your sacral chakra, imagine that the cloud is now orange—breathe in the color slowly, and let it fill your lungs and flow throughout this chakra. Breathe the color out through this center, and continue with the remaining chakras. At the very end, imagine a very bright white light. Slowly breathe it in, and hold for a moment. As you release the breath, see a gray mist leaving you that contains all your tension, worries, and negativity.

Take some time at the end of this exercise to feel what it's like to have all your chakras balanced and glowing with spectral light. You are a rainbow!

Chakra Sounds

Have you ever noticed people chanting different tones while they're sitting in meditation? Well, what they're doing is charging up and vibrating their chakra system. Since each of the seven main chakras has its own unique frequency and vibration, using sound with them can be a powerfully energizing and invigorating experience. It can also help stimulate and enhance your physical energy level.

Exercise

By chanting the following sounds of each chakra, you'll balance and encourage the flow of energy to each center. This technique is another great way of heightening your psychic awareness, and it only takes as little as five minutes (of course you may take longer if you wish).

Here are the corresponding sounds to each chakra:

Chakra	Sound
Base	*Lam*
Sacral	*Vam*
Solar plexus	*Ram*
Heart	*Yam*
Throat	*Ham*
Third eye	*Om*
Crown	*Silence*

Each of the above sounds that have an "a" in them are in fact pronounced with a short-sounding "u," and the sound is meant to be elongated and held at the end. For example, *Lam* is pronounced and chanted *luuuummmmmmmmm, Vam* is pronounced and chanted *vuuuummmmmmm,* and so on.

In your mind's eye, imagine that you're seeing the color of your first chakra; as you do so, slowly start to chant its corresponding sound, *Lam.* Keep your attention there until you've completely sounded out the appropriate chant sound. Continue to move up through all your chakras while you imagine the color for each one and chant each chakra sound. When you get to the crown chakra, just be still: Enjoy the heightened vibration and relish the calming silence for a few moments.

This uplifting meditation can help anytime you need a quick energy boost.

Affirmations:

"I am a rainbow of psychic energy."

*"Every day I take a moment to
balance and cleanse my spiritual batteries."*

Raising the Power

Your psychic ability is intricately linked to the chakras, so it's possible to stimulate your psychic centers purely by thought. However, too much psychic work or even talking about psychic matters can open you up and may make you feel tired, moody, or even irritable—keeping yourself cleansed, protected, and closed down properly will help and become important practices in your personal development. Don't forget that you're a spiritual being living in a physical body, and each deserves a 50-50 split of your time and devotion. In this way, you'll be able to stay grounded and balanced so that your spirit and body can live and work together in harmony. Your inner guidance is just a part of you . . . it isn't *all* of you.

When you fully open your chakras, you'll also expand your auric field. As I explained earlier, when this happens you'll become more susceptible to all vibrations around you; consequently, you'll begin to notice how sensitive you're becoming. You're likely to become more attuned to everyone and everything.

I mentioned earlier that when I read for private clients or speak onstage, I feel *everything:* the people on the Other Side, those around me in the audience, and my own feelings. It's as though every sense is being bombarded, but charged with emotion. Fortunately, I've learned how to deal with this influx of feelings, close down, and manage the process. The nature of my work means that I'm often open and highly sensitive, so I find that too much time in big cities can often tip the scales into psychic overload. The frenzied movement, noise, and hustle can be too much for my senses for prolonged periods. So I now live in the country, where the pace of life is slower, the earth grounds me, and I have time to meditate, exercise, and maintain a healthy, balanced life. I know firsthand how important it is to take care of yourself when you're developing and operating your psychic equipment.

In this last, essential exercise, we'll be working with all the major chakras. Try to imagine each of the seven centers as a small, colored, bright light. As you visualize these lights growing and shrinking in size, you'll be opening and closing your chakras. This practice will not only infuse your chakras with vitality and energy, but as with some of the other exercises, it will also heighten and expand your psychic awareness.

As before, you'll start off with the base chakra and work your way up to the crown chakra; and keep in mind that the base and crown chakras should always remain *open* and *balanced,* allowing you to be a conduit for precious life-giving energy to flow properly throughout your entire system, physically as well as spiritually. Using the image of a colored light for each chakra, along with just sending the thought to open and close each one, will often be enough to raise and amplify your psychic power.

Although this exercise is quite powerful—and I know how much you want to begin with this part of your development—there are some important rules to follow: (1) Open your chakras in sequence; (2) be aware of each chakra; and (3) close down each chakra properly.

Okay, let's begin.

Exercise

Begin by sitting down with your spine straight, and get comfortable. Take a few slow Complete Breaths in and out; relax. Now I want you to visualize a red light at the base of your spine. See the light begin to expand and grow in size. As it does, imagine that there's a brilliant white light coming up from the earth through the soles of your feet, up your legs, and eventually merging with the red light at your base chakra. Take your time here—this exercise is highly powerful and shouldn't be rushed.

Since the chakras are connected, I'd like you to now visualize a small orange light in your sacral center and see it begin to slowly expand and grow in size. As before, bring up the white light again; but this time, it should move *through* your red base chakra, and into your orange sacral chakra. Continue to do this one by one with all your chakras—and always bring up the white light from the earth, through your base chakra, and then through all your chakras one by one in sequential order. Your breath will help raise the energy to each center.

Once you've opened all the chakras, take just a moment to run the energy from your spine right up to the top of your crown chakra. Take note of this amazing feeling, in which all your centers are open and pulsating simultaneously. Now place your awareness on your crown chakra and imagine that there's a big funnel reaching out to the universe. This time, see a *new* bright-white light begin to form above and slowly pour down through this center, as it meets and merges with the white light from below. Allow these two white lights to blend and become one, and let the intensity of light fill your psychic centers with even more energy. Take a moment to notice how your aura expands naturally so that you feel as though all the natural boundaries just disappear. This is what's known as *being open.*

You can remain this way until you're ready to start the closing-down process. Once again, you're going to use the power of thought to close down each chakra, one by one. When you're ready, let the white light from above continue to pour through your crown chakra, which remains open. Now bring your awareness to your third-eye chakra. Make the expanded indigo light (the corresponding color) smaller and smaller—you should feel the power begin to diminish as you move down to your throat chakra and its pale-blue light. Focus on this light getting smaller, and then move on down to the heart, solar-plexus, and sacral centers. All the different colored lights should be smaller now, resulting in what's known as *being closed.* (But remember that you need to keep the crown and base chakras open for a continued flow of energy throughout your system.)

Opening and closing your psychic centers is an essential exercise if you wish to continue to safely develop your psychic and intuitive abilities—there's no way around it. This is the number one exercise that I've learned and now teach regularly in my workshops. I also use it myself, before and after all psychic work. (Additionally, the CD included in this book will guide you through a more enhanced version of this exercise, and will assist you in your ongoing journey toward true inner awareness.)

Affirmations:

"I am pulsating with psychic energy."
"I open and close all my energy centers properly and efficiently."

CHAPTER

Psychic
Tools for Life

L iving a psychic life is an ongoing process of perpetual development, one of learning to trust and listen to your inner guidance. You must accept that life is your ultimate teacher and try to live to the very best of your abilities—after all, what you do with what you have is what truly matters. And since we're all uniquely different in how we interpret signals and receive guidance, I urge you to seek your own experiences so that you acquire your own awareness. In turn, you'll be able to make up your own mind about which spiritual path you want to follow, and you can then assemble your own psychic toolbox.

Intuitive or psychic information can sometimes come from out of the blue, as if it has a mind of its own. It may be the answer to a question you asked days ago; or you could be taking a shower, drying your hair, driving to pick up the kids from school, or raking the leaves when intuitive information registers in your conscious mind. No matter how you receive it, when you follow your inner guidance, choices and decisions seem to flow smoothly. Remember how it felt to follow a hunch that you just knew was right? You were probably pretty excited, and might have even felt a positive charge surge through your body as synchronicities and coincidences seemed to just guide you toward your goal. On the other hand, when you ignore your inner guidance, a feeling of stagnation can occur—life can appear to be out of sync and discordant, and you're *not* likely to feel that positive charge surrounding your actions.

In this chapter, I want to provide you with some final techniques that you can incorporate into all areas of your life. (Once you've learned them, I'm sure that you'll go on to create more of your own.) Most of them only take a few minutes, so you'll be able to tap in to your abilities instantly and effortlessly, no matter where you are or what you're doing. These exercises are for times when you're not able to do a full meditation or you can't wait until conditions are perfect—they're meant to jump-start you into using your newfound inner guidance.

You can now start to navigate your own psychic path, lead a life of fullness and purpose, and show the world how amazing you really are!

Decision Making

Making decisions doesn't necessarily come naturally to everyone—after all, we live in a world where it's easy to get someone else to make them for us. Of course, there are some things we should just leave to the experts, but I'm talking about those determinations we're capable of making if we just tap in to our inner guidance. When we make a decision based on intuition, we trust our feelings, and when this happens for the first time, it's like a turning point—from that moment on, our confidence builds and we don't look back!

We must acknowledge, honor, and act upon these feelings and signs that try to point us in the right direction. For example, I remember a time not too long ago when I was about to give a demonstration where the organizers were expecting a large audience. Several days before, I kept getting a nagging feeling to call them and make sure that everything was okay, and to check that they had all the sound equipment for the evening. Instead, my rational mind kicked in and said, "No, John, they're professionals who have done this hundreds of times before. Let it go."

Even though I'm a psychic medium, I don't always pay attention to *everything* I feel (hey, I'm human after all).

Of course I arrived to find that the place had a broken microphone system, a child's stool (only 12 inches high) for me to perch on, and no air-conditioning on this muggy New England night, when the temperature was still 89 degrees. And the spotlight had enough juice coming from it to light up New York City! I should have honored and trusted my feelings earlier and followed through with the decision to call the organizers of this event—by doing so, I could have saved a lot of aggravation for myself and the staff who rushed around trying to fix everything.

I'm sure you can identify with what I went through. In fact, you've no doubt found yourself hesitating to make decisions because you're afraid of the risks and the end result, which you've probably already imagined. I know it's scary to listen to your intuition when your logic is dragging you in the opposite direction, but fear will hold you prisoner if you let it. Remember that your intuition isn't meant to replace reason; instead, it's meant to *enhance* your logic, thereby giving you a far better chance to succeed.

Keep in mind that your body will tell you when you're following your intuition, and it's crucial that you interpret your own feelings when making some type of decision. Some people feel a flutter when something feels wrong; others feel a tingling sensation all over if they're on the right path; while still others feel nothing when they're not supposed to move ahead.

I have a friend who uses his own simple technique when he has to make a decision that he's not totally sure about: He takes a few moments and imagines a simple streetlight in front of him. He then asks a question about the decision and watches to see if the light changes: Red means stop, yellow means wait, and green means proceed. Of course, he's not really getting the answer from a traffic light, but is using his own personal symbol to tap in to his inner guidance.

I also know of some people who have trained themselves to imagine a *yes* in one hand and *no* in the other. They ask a question and wait to see what hand rises, whether it's the yes hand or the no hand. (But sometimes this isn't so simple. I once did a workshop where the students wrote one question that would require a yes or no response and placed it in an envelope. The envelopes were then distributed to the students, who didn't know whose question they now held in their hands. One student started to use her awareness in the exercise and came up with a definite *yes*, but she also saw a swinging bridge suspended over a deep valley. The student felt that the person whose question was in the envelope could achieve their goal, but it wouldn't be an easy one. They'd have to hang on and work through other issues as they continued to move forward toward this desired outcome. The question in the envelope was, "Should I move residences?" The student who asked the question raised her hand and thanked the other student. She agreed that the new move for her might have been great, but what about her feelings concerning finding a new job or moving away from her family?

My colleague Lynn Robinson, who's a business consultant, teaches intuitive techniques to Fortune 500 company executives and their employees. Some of these people have never worked with their sixth sense before, so they find it difficult to articulate their experience—they don't realize the rich resource of information that can accessed through their intuition. Lynn teaches them to imagine the decisions and choices in front of them, one by one—from "Should I proceed with this project?" to "Is this person right for the job?" to "Should I hire more staff?" Then Lynn has them ask themselves, "How do I feel about this decision?" and "If I make this decision, how will I feel about it six months or a year from now?" Like me, Lynn encourages her clients to notice how their body feels: Does it feel light, heavy, or tense? Are there any colors, symbols, or words they're sensing? She then asks them to write down what they're receiving *before* their rational mind tries to influence the outcome. Once the group has committed these initial feelings to paper, they have a new way to look at the information from an intuitive perspective. Lynn then finishes up by teaching everyone how to interpret the information for themselves, and shows them that all their future decisions can be guided for the best positive outcome if they simply just *pause* and *ask* for guidance.

Remember that your psychic abilities are part of you, so use *all* of yourself when you feel you need a little assistance or Divine guidance. You don't always have to turn over your power to someone else when it comes to making decisions. With practice, you'll learn how to interpret your own specific signs. *Please* begin with small decisions and choices so that you can build up your trust and confidence gradually. Have faith in your inner guidance, which is always there and waiting for you to ask it for help—it wants nothing more than the best for you.

Affirmations:

"I remember to pause and ask before I act."
"I trust my Divine guidance in all areas of my life."

Psychometry

During my years of training, I came upon the word *psychometry* (which means "measure of the soul") so many times that I decided to read whatever I could on the subject.

I found out that it's the practice of holding someone's personal possession and then reading it—a way of somehow seeing through touch. This a great tool to use as you develop your awareness, as its benefits will help you reach beyond your five physical senses by tuning down your conscious mind and reaching a psychic level.

Remember what I've said all through this book: Everything is made up of energy. This includes your favorite ring, that old shirt you're wearing, or the chair you're sitting in right now. Think about it: Have you ever borrowed someone's shirt or sweater and noticed that it made you feel different? What's happening here is that you're picking up that person's emotions and their essence.

I have a friend who uses psychometry every time she gets a new contract or a business card. She stops, holds the paper or card, and tunes in to see if she's feeling positive or negative—which helps her make the right business decision. I've also used this technique with flowers: By just holding a stem that someone else has held, I'm able to feel the energy that passed between the two living things.

While in the UK, I attended the Arthur Findlay College (which I discussed in my first book, *Born Knowing*). This is where flower clairsentience was introduced to me. While in class, our instructor would arrange some flowers that each student had brought in a vase, although we had no idea of who had brought which blossom. We'd then choose the one that we were most attracted to. Holding the flower, we'd use psychometry to read for the person who had brought it in. We were establishing a strong link with each other—and often with those on the Other Side, too. It was as if holding a beautiful rose was a way to open the door into another world.

Exercise

Hopefully by now you've worked through all the exercises in this book and have established your psychic strength(s), whether it's clairsentience, clairvoyance, or clairaudience. I want you to practice by holding something that someone else really values. (It's best if you didn't know the person whose item you'll be using, since you'll want to be totally objective and keep your thoughts out of the process altogether.)

Now focus on the appropriate chakra (depending on your psychic strength) while you hold the object. You don't need to grip it tightly, just hold it lightly in your right hand (if you're left-handed, hold it in your left hand). Keep turning it around in your hand, as the images and feelings begin to form. Write down the first few things that come to mind, but *don't* analyze or give your mind a chance to shoot down what you're receiving. Ask questions as you hold the object, such as: Is this person married? Do they have children? Are they happy? What do they do for a living? What advice can I give to help them right now? (There's no limit to the amount of questions you can ask.)

Share what you received, whether it's feelings, words, images, or symbols, with the owner of the object. You might be amazed with what you received, and how it translates into fact.

Affirmations:

"I am safely beginning to develop my psychometric abilities."
"My hands are receptors for psychic energy."

Energy Scanning

Our psychic energy is a precious resource that has the ability to help us in any given situation. Using this energy, we can learn to blend with anyone or anything. I notice this particularly when I teach my workshops. Most people walk in thinking that they don't have a psychic bone in their body—but the first thing I tell them is that we're *all* "born knowing." I explain that they just need to experiment and reach into themselves to recover what they once knew.

Next, I usually start off with a lighthearted warm-up exercise in which I ask if there's someone in the group who has a scar that's hidden from view to come up to the front of the room. I then take the group through the exercise that follows and ask them to "see," "feel," or "hear" where the scar is. I go around and ask them one by one where they feel the scarred area is—and amazingly, more than 75 percent of the class will correctly guess the right area. Yet I'm fascinated by the fact that the other 25 percent feel different things. I remember one workshop when a student kept seeing sinus issues with the volunteer, who insisted that she didn't suffer from any problems in that area. Sure enough, a week later the volunteer picked up a nasty sinus infection. In this case, the student sensed an energy disturbance before it actually manifested in the volunteer's body.

This technique has many uses—for example, you can try scanning a highway or road for traffic before you're immersed in it. It can also assist you in determining how you get your intuitive information. For example, my student Judy uses her own form of scanning to find her husband every time they go into a department store. She stops, expands her aura, and waits to see if she's pulled to a certain area, or if an image or symbol enters her mind, such as a TV, a stereo, a basketball, or a hammer. When she sees the image in her mind's eye, she goes right to the appropriate department.

Medical intuitives have trained themselves with this technique to assist in sensing where blockages occur in their patients. (I believe that, in the future, more psychics and intuitives will work side by side with the medical community.) It's also a great tool for mothers; and I even know of people who scan used products before purchasing them—

sometimes they'll see a flaw that's not visible to their naked eye. The opportunities are endless!

Try the following simple exercise so that you can put energy scanning to practical use for yourself.

Exercise

Have a friend stand in front of you; or better yet, have your friend bring someone you've never met before to see you. Stand about a foot or two apart from the other person, close your eyes, and imagine that you're both made of pure light—then visualize your energy field blending with his. Let your awareness sweep up and down his body in long, slow movements. See if there's one particular spot where your attention is drawn. Can you see any colors, or is one part brighter than another? Take your time, and make a mental note of everything you're feeling.

Now open your eyes and tell him what you've received. As always, you may want to write down your experience in your journal so that you can continue to build up your visual symbols, feelings, and interpretations. *Please remember* that when you deliver the information, you have to take responsibility for how you present it. I was taught that when you get an *impression,* you should be careful of your *expression*—you don't want to scare anyone, especially if you're a beginner.

By practicing this exercise frequently, you'll soon realize that energy scanning is a tool that you can hone and use anytime. (And best of all, it's quick!)

Affirmations:

"I am more than this physical body."

"Everyone and everything is made of energy, and we are all connected."

Your Psychic Time

Here's a scenario you're probably all too familiar with: You get up, take a shower, eat breakfast, get dressed, and go off to work, all the while trying to feel positive and hoping for a great day. You hit heavy traffic (or the bus or train is crowded), you remember the kids forgot their lunches, and finally you look down to realize that you're currently wearing your cup of coffee. Your stress and anxiety levels have risen to critical levels before you even get to work. So if you don't stop, breathe, and check in with yourself, the rest of day will most likely be crazy, leaving you scrambling to catch up. And obviously, if your body and mind are stressed, it's that much harder to acknowledge and listen to your intuition. But one of my students doesn't settle for "living" like this.

Debra has a high-paced job, and she's always on the go. From the moment she wakes up until she gets home and kicks off her shoes, she makes important business decisions for her company and depends on her inner guidance to help with those decisions, thus ensuring that her day hums along as smoothly as possible. Every morning before she even gets her coffee or greets her colleagues, she goes into her office, closes the door, mutes the phone, and doesn't look at her computer or e-mail. She performs her own psychic check-in for just ten minutes. By doing so, Debra is able to begin her workday feeling balanced, confident, and calm— she knows what's coming up, and she's prepared for it. Intuitive information has a better chance of getting her attention when she begins each day by simply turning inward and taking a few minutes for herself and her intuition.

The moral of this story is simple: Try to start off every day in a prepared, positive frame of mind and get connected to your inner guidance *before* the external world gets ahold of you. But will you give yourself the opportunity? The choice is always yours. . . .

Exercise

I recommend that you try this last exercise in the morning. Whether you do it before you go to work, or you decide to go in a little earlier and practice it at the office, is up to you. By doing this short exercise, you'll begin to build a relationship with your inner guidance, one that can be accessed when *you* need it.

Begin by closing your eyes and taking a Complete Breath.

Begin to relax—let your awareness bring you back into your body, and follow your breath into the quiet place within your heart. Take a few breaths into this area, and continue to relax and feel more grounded. Your body and mind will begin to grow quieter with each breath. Next, bring your awareness into your solar-plexus area, and ask your intuition if there's anything specific it wants to tell you. Breathe and pause here for a moment, taking whatever comes. Now guide your awareness up to your crown chakra, and ask if there's a situation that you should know about or that would be helpful for the coming day. Depending on your psychic strength, you may receive words, symbols, or a feeling about what you need or want to know.

It doesn't take long to do this exercise, and you may receive something important, something quite small, or nothing at all. At least you're honoring yourself and your inner guidance by making the commitment to listen. After a while, you'll see how your days seem to flow better with a sense of guidance and enthusiasm. People around you may notice the changes and might even inquire how you seem to know what to do in any given situation.

Affirmations:

"I am psychic."
"Every day and in every way, I take a moment to listen within."

About the
Meditation CD

The CD accompanying this book includes two special meditations. The first is a short one called "Healing Relaxation for Body & Mind," in which I'll guide you through the process to relax your body and clear your mind. The benefits of this meditation will make it easier for you to let go of stress and to experience improved relaxation, patience, concentration, calmness, and tranquility. You can do this short meditation independently, or you can use it as a preparation for the longer meditation.

In the second meditation, entitled "Raising the Power," I'll guide you through a deep meditation to enhance your intuitive psychic abilities. Throughout, I'll also instruct you how to open and raise your energy safely and efficiently through all the chakras, how to open and expand your aura, and how to make yourself more receptive to psychic information. At the end of the meditation, I'll guide you through the process to contract your aura and close down your psychic centers. Proper opening and closing of one's psychic centers is vital to all psychic work, and of course, it will assist you on a physical level.

Before you listen to this CD, I highly recommend that you become familiar with the text in this book first so that you have a better understanding of the breath, chakras, and auras. This will then enhance the benefits and experience of the meditation CD even more.

So all that's left is to let my meditations assist you in navigating and charting your path, which leads to your inner guidance—and to the spirit within all of us.

Enjoy the journey.

Afterword

t's now time to start using your inner guidance and to give yourself permission to let it assist, guide, and show you any- and everything that's possible. It will help you navigate your life's path, and it will be a constant companion for your soul's journey. After all, you have *all* the equipment you need to live an intuitive life and tap in to the inner guidance system that's always been with you—no matter how many times you've ignored it or didn't pay attention to its voice.

I hope that by now you've learned and understood the mechanics of your psychic abilities and how they work and function for you. I wrote this book to show you where to find your personal set of keys that can open doors that you may not have thought of opening, or those you're afraid to look into. Some of you may choose to step through those magical doors and get to know and work with your inner guidance; as a result, you'll immediately become attuned to your body, mind, and spirit. But it's okay if you decide to enter at another time—your psychic abilities will be there waiting. All they want is that you honor them by simply asking for their guidance, and that you reacquaint yourself with the God-given gift that is your birthright.

Remember that you must have responsibility when it comes to using your psychic abilities. Most important, proceed slowly and stay balanced, keeping in mind that you have to honor *all* of you—physically, emotionally, mentally, and spiritually. You've chosen a unique path that should never be forced upon anyone else—it's your path, with your nametag on it. When the time is right, others around you may begin to question things outside themselves, and hopefully, they'll also look inward to find their own answers.

It's been my pleasure to work with you throughout this book, and I have just one last wish for each and every one of you: May your life be filled with love, abundance, new adventures, and constant learning, and may it be one of extraordinary discoveries.

God bless, and I wish you well.

The End

Recommended Resources

Andrews, Ted. *How to See and Read the Aura,* Llewellyn, 1991.

Fontana, David. *Learn to Meditate,* Chronicle Books, 1999.

Friends of the Western Buddhist Order, *Mindfulness of Breathing.*

Gawain, Shakti. *Developing Intuition,* New World Library, 2000.

Judith, Anodea, Ph.D. *Wheels of Life,* Llewellyn, 1999.

Lawson, David. *Your Psychic Potential,* Thorsons, 1997.

Northage, Ivy. *Mediumship Made Simple,* Light Publishing, 1986.

Parker-Hamilton, Craig and Jane. *The Psychic Workbook,* Vermilion, 1995.

Ramacharaka, Yogi. *Science of Breath,* Yogi Publication Society, 1904.

Roberts, Billy. *Master Your Psychic Powers,* Blanford, 1998.

Robinson, Lynn A. *Compass of the Soul,* Andrews McMeel, 2003.

Sanders, Jr., Pete A. *You Are Psychic,* Fawcett Columbine, 1989.

Toy, Fiona. *Auras and Chakras,* Barnes and Noble, 2002.

Wanless, James. *Intuition @ Work,* Red Wheel, 2002.

Weed, Joseph J. *Psychic Energy,* Parker Publishing, 1970.

Acknowledgments

I really do believe that people come into our lives for a reason, to help put us on the path we were born to follow—or even to help us pave the way. I'm honored to have written and have my name on this, my second book, which I could only have accomplished with the help and support of the following friends and colleagues:

I wish to thank the dedicated, tireless support and patience of my friend Simon, who helped me shape and edit this book. (You are truly a sculptor of words.) Thank you to my assistant, Gretchen, and to my entire support team, all of whom play their own important part in helping me. Without their help, I wouldn't have been able to focus so much time on *Psychic Navigator.*

I'd also like to acknowledge the support of my publishing company, Hay House, and the team that continues to spread enlightenment and the word throughout the world. They've been a pleasure to work with in each country.

Finally, I'm blessed with a phenomenal group of friends and colleagues who have inspired me to continue writing and have been my constant support. This includes: my family and extended family for their support and for believing in me; my literary agent, John Willig; Debbie and Josh; Lynn Robinson; Gary Watson; Brian and Carol Weiss; Cathy Copeland; Kate and Yanik; Bob and Melissa Olson; Suzane Northrop; John Edward; Cathy at Circles of Wisdom; Dilek Mir; Chris and Paul; Joyce; Judy Guggenheim; Craig Hughes; Josie and Des; Mei-Mei; Fran; Darlene Bethoney; Jennifer V.; Lorna B.; Vincent J. Barra; and so many others. Thank you all for your kindness and support, and for being there for me.

About the Author

John Holland is an internationally renowned psychic medium who has been lecturing, demonstrating, and reading for private clients for more than 15 years. He's dedicated to his ongoing personal development, which inspires him to continue teaching.

John says, "If I can help people connect with someone on the Other Side, and bring peace, comfort, and perhaps some closure to them, then I feel I've done my job. But mediumship is more than just delivering messages: It's about the confirmation that once our physical body dies, our spirit lives on; and it's about how the spirits of our relatives, friends, and loved ones are still connected to us."

John is eager to promote the difference between a *psychic* and a *medium:* A psychic can draw information from your aura, which can provide knowledge about both current and future events, whereas a medium is the conduit between the spirit world and the physical world—a "soul-to-soul connection," as John so often calls it.

For further information about John and his series of workshops and events, visit: **www.johnholland.com**, or write to:

John Holland
P.O. Box 561
Newmarket, NH 03857

John's *FREE* e-mailed newsletter includes tips
on developing your psychic and intuitive abilities,
interviews with other authors, book reviews and helpful
Website links. To get your free quarterly newsletter, sign
up online to join John's e-mail newsletter list (where it
says "sign up now" at the base of the homepage on
www.johnholland.com).

We hope you enjoyed this Hay House book.
If you'd like to receive a free catalog featuring additional
Hay House books and products, or if you'd like information
about the Hay Foundation, please contact:

Hay House, Inc.
P.O. Box 5100
Carlsbad, CA 92018-5100

(760) 431-7695 or **(800) 654-5126**
(760) 431-6948 (fax) or **(800) 650-5115 (fax)**
www.hayhouse.com • www.hayfoundation.org

Published and distributed in Australia by:
Hay House Australia Pty. Ltd., 18/36 Ralph St., Alexandria NSW
2015 • *Phone:* 612-9669-4299 • *Fax:* 612-9669-4144
www.hayhouse.com.au

Published and distributed in the United Kingdom by:
Hay House UK, Ltd., 292B Kensal Rd., London W10 5BE
Phone: 44-20-8962-1230 • *Fax:* 44-20-8962-1239
www.hayhouse.co.uk

Published and distributed in the Republic of South Africa by: Hay House SA (Pty), Ltd., P.O. Box 990, Witkoppen 2068
Phone/Fax: 27-11-467-8904 • orders@psdprom.co.za
www.hayhouse.co.za

Published in India by: Hay House Publishers India, Muskaan Complex, Plot No. 3, B-2, Vasant Kunj, New Delhi 110 070
Phone: 91-11-4176-1620 • *Fax:* 91-11-4176-1630
www.hayhouse.co.in

Distributed in Canada by: Raincoast,
9050 Shaughnessy St., Vancouver, B.C. V6P 6E5
Phone: (604) 323-7100 • *Fax:* (604) 323-2600
www.raincoast.com

⌧ ⌧ ⌧

Tune in to **HayHouseRadio.com**® for the best in inspirational talk radio featuring top Hay House authors! And, sign up via the Hay House USA Website to receive the Hay House online newsletter and stay informed about what's going on with your favorite authors. You'll receive bimonthly announcements about Discounts and Offers, Special Events, Product Highlights, Free Excerpts, Giveaways, and more!
www.hayhouse.com®